5 Accuplacer Math Practice Tests

Extra Practice to Help Achieve an Excellent Score

By

Reza Nazari

All inquiries should be addressed to:
info@effortlessMath.com
www.EffortlessMath.com

ISBN: 978-1-64612-250-9

Published by: **Effortless Math Education Inc.**

For Online Math Practice Visit www.EffortlessMath.com

Welcome to

Accuplacer Math Prep
2021

Thank you for choosing Effortless Math for your Accuplacer Math test preparation and congratulations on making the decision to take the Accuplacer test! It's a remarkable move you are taking, one that shouldn't be diminished in any capacity. That's why you need to use every tool possible to ensure you succeed on the test with the highest possible score, and this extensive practice book is one such tool.

If math has never been a strong subject for you, **don't worry**! This book will help you prepare for (and even ACE) the Accuplacer test's math section. As test day draws nearer, effective preparation becomes increasingly more important. Thankfully, you have this comprehensive practice book to help you get ready for the test. With this book, you can feel confident that you will be more than ready for the Accuplacer Math test when the time comes.

First and foremost, it is important to note that this book is a practice book and not a prep book. Every test of this "self-guided math practice book" was carefully developed to ensure that you are making the most effective use of your time while preparing for the test. This up-to-date guide reflects the 2021 test guidelines and will put you on the right track to hone your math skills, overcome exam anxiety, and boost your confidence, so that you can have your best to succeed on the Accuplacer Math test.

This practice book will:

☑ Explain the format of the Accuplacer Math test.

☑ Describe specific test-taking strategies that you can use on the test.

☑ Provide Accuplacer Math test-taking tips.

☑ Help you identify the areas in which you need to concentrate your study time.

☑ Offer Accuplacer Math questions and explanations to help you develop the basic math skills.

☑ Give **realistic and full-length practice tests** (featuring new question types) with detailed answers to help you measure your exam readiness and build confidence.

This practice book contains 5 practice tests to help you succeed on the Accuplacer Math test. You'll get in-depth instructions on every math topic as well as tips and techniques on how to answer each question type. You'll also get plenty of practice questions to boost your test-taking confidence.

In addition, in the following pages you'll find:

➢ **How to Use This Book Effectively** – This section provides you with step-by-step instructions on how to get the most out of this comprehensive practice book.

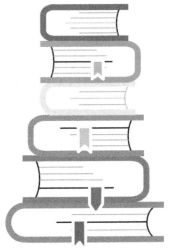

➢ **How to study for the Accuplacer Math Test** – A six-step study program has been developed to help you make the best use of this book and prepare for your Accuplacer Math test. Here you'll find tips and strategies to guide your study program and help you understand Accuplacer Math and how to ace the test.

➢ **Accuplacer Math Review** – Learn everything you need to know about the Accuplacer Math test.

➢ **Accuplacer Math Test-Taking Strategies** – Learn how to effectively put these recommended test-taking techniques into use for improving your Accuplacer Math score.

➢ **Test Day Tips** – Review these tips to make sure you will do your best when the big day comes.

Effortless Math's Accuplacer Online Center

Effortless Math Online Accuplacer Center offers a complete study program, including the following:

✓ Step-by-step instructions on how to prepare for the Accuplacer Math test

✓ Numerous Accuplacer Math worksheets to help you measure your math skills

✓ Complete list of Accuplacer Math formulas

✓ Video lessons for all Accuplacer Math topics

✓ Full-length Accuplacer Math practice tests

✓ And much more…

No Registration Required.

Visit **EffortlessMath.com/Accuplacer** to find your online Accuplacer Math resources.

How to Use This Book Effectively

Look no further when you need a practice book to improve your math skills to succeed on the math portion of the Accuplacer test. Each section of this comprehensive practice book will provide you with the knowledge, tools, and understanding needed to succeed on the test.

It's imperative that you understand each practice question before moving onto another one, as that's the way to guarantee your success. Each practice test provides you with a step-by-step guide of every question to better understand the content that will be on the test. To get the best possible results from this book:

➢ **Begin studying long before your test date**.
This provides you ample time to learn the different math concepts. The earlier you begin studying for the test, the sharper your skills will be. Do not procrastinate! Provide yourself with plenty of time to learn the concepts and feel comfortable that you understand them when your test date arrives.

➢ **Practice consistently**. Study Accuplacer Math concepts at least 20 to 30 minutes a day. Remember, slow and steady wins the race, which can be applied to preparing for the Accuplacer Math test. Instead of cramming to tackle everything at once, be patient and learn the math topics in short bursts.

➢ Whenever you get a math problem wrong, **mark it off, and review it later** to make sure you understand the concept.

➢ Once you've reviewed the book's instructions, **take a practice test** to gauge your level of readiness. Then, review your results. Read detailed answers and solutions for each question you missed.

➢ **Take another practice test** to get an idea of how ready you are to take the actual exam. Taking the practice tests will give you the confidence you need on test day. Simulate the Accuplacer testing environment by sitting in a quiet room free from distraction. Make sure to clock yourself with a timer.

How to Study for the Accuplacer Math Test

Studying for the Accuplacer Math test can be a really daunting and boring task. What's the best way to go about it? Is there a certain study method that works better than others? Well, studying for the Accuplacer Math can be done effectively. The following six-step program has been designed to make preparing for the Accuplacer Math test more efficient and less overwhelming.

Step 1 - Create a study plan

Step 2 - Choose your study resources

Step 3 - Review, Learn, Practice

Step 4 - Learn and practice test-taking strategies

Step 5 - Learn the Accuplacer Test format and take practice tests

Step 6 - Analyze your performance

STEP 1: Create a Study Plan

It's always easier to get things done when you have a plan. Creating a study plan for the Accuplacer Math test can help you to stay on track with your studies. It's important to sit down and prepare a study plan with what works with your life, work, and any other obligations you may have. Devote enough time each day to studying. It's also a 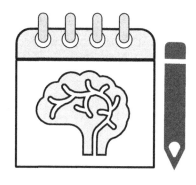 great idea to break down each section of the exam into blocks and study one concept at a time.

It's important to understand that there is no "right" way to create a study plan. Your study plan will be personalized based on your specific needs and learning style.

Follow these guidelines to create an effective study plan for your Accuplacer Math test:

★ **Analyze your learning style and study habits** – Everyone has a different learning style. It is essential to embrace your individuality and the unique way you learn. Think about what works and what doesn't work for you. Do you prefer Accuplacer Math prep books or a combination of textbooks and video lessons? Does it work better for you if you study every night for thirty minutes or is it more effective to study in the morning before going to work?

★ **Evaluate your schedule** – Review your current schedule and find out how much time you can consistently devote to Accuplacer Math study.

★ **Develop a schedule** – Now it's time to add your study schedule to your calendar like any other obligation. Schedule time for study, practice, and review. Plan out which topic you will study on which day to ensure that you're devoting enough time to each concept. Develop a study plan that is mindful, realistic, and flexible.

★ **Stick to your schedule** – A study plan is only effective when it is followed consistently. You should try to develop a study plan that you can follow for the length of your study program.

★ **Evaluate your study plan and adjust as needed** – Sometimes you need to adjust your plan when you have new commitments. Check in with yourself regularly to make sure that you're not falling behind in your study plan. Remember, the most important thing is sticking to your plan. Your study plan is all about helping you be more productive. If you find that your study plan is not as effective as you want, don't get discouraged. It's okay to make changes as you figure out what works best for you.

STEP 2: Choose Your Study Resources

There are numerous textbooks and online resources available for the Accuplacer Math test, and it may not be clear where to begin. Don't worry! Effortless Math's Accuplacer online center provides everything you need to fully prepare for your Accuplacer Math test. In addition to the practice tests in this book, you can also use Effortless Math's online resources. (video lessons, worksheets, formulas, etc.)

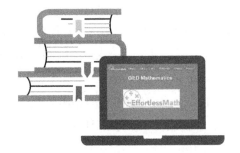

Simply visit EffortlessMath.com/Accuplacer to find your online Accuplacer Math resources.

STEP 3: Review, Learn, Practice

Effortless Math's Accuplacer course breaks down each subject into specific skills or content areas. For instance, the percent concept is separated into different topics—percent calculation, percent increase and decrease, percent problems, etc. Use our online resources to help you go over all key math concepts and topics on the Accuplacer Math test.

As you review each concept, take notes or highlight the concepts you would like to go over again in the future. If you're unfamiliar with a topic or something is difficult for you, do additional research on it. For each math topic, plenty of instructions, step-by-step guides, and examples are provided to ensure you get a good grasp of the material. You can also find video lessons on the Effortless Math website for each Accuplacer Math concept.

Quickly review the topics you do understand to get a brush-up of the material. Be sure to use the worksheets and do the practice questions provided on the Effortless Math's online center to measure your understanding of the concepts.

STEP 4: Learn and Practice Test-taking Strategies

In the following sections, you will find important test-taking strategies and tips that can help you earn extra points. You'll learn how to think strategically and when to guess if you don't know the answer to a question. Using Accuplacer Math test-taking strategies and tips can help you raise your score and do well on the test. Apply test taking strategies on the practice tests to help you boost your confidence.

STEP 5: Learn the Accuplacer Test Format and Take Practice Tests

The Accuplacer *Test Review* section provides information about the structure of the Accuplacer test. Read this section to learn more about the Accuplacer test structure, different test sections, the number of questions in each section, and the section time limits. When you have a prior understanding of the test format and different types of Accuplacer Math questions, you'll feel more confident when you take the actual exam.

Once you have read through the instructions and lessons and feel like you are ready to go – take advantage of the full-length Accuplacer Math practice tests available in this book. Use the practice tests to sharpen your skills and build confidence.

The Accuplacer Math practice tests offered in the book are formatted similarly to the actual Accuplacer Math test. When you take each practice test, try to simulate actual testing conditions. To take the practice tests, sit in a quiet space, time yourself, and work through as many of the questions as time allows. The practice tests are followed by detailed answer explanations to help you find your weak areas, learn from your mistakes, and raise your Accuplacer Math score.

STEP 6: Analyze Your Performance

After taking the practice tests, look over the answer keys and explanations to learn which questions you answered correctly and which you did not. Never be discouraged if you make a few mistakes. See them as a learning opportunity. This will highlight your strengths and weaknesses.

You can use the results to determine if you need additional practice or if you are ready to take the actual Accuplacer Math test.

Looking for more?

Visit EffortlessMath.com/Accuplacer to find hundreds of Accuplacer Math worksheets, video tutorials, practice tests, Accuplacer Math formulas, and much more.

Or scan this QR code.

No Registration Required.

Accuplacer Test Review

The Next-Generation ACCUPLACER test is an assessment system for measuring students' readiness for college courses in reading, writing, and mathematics. The test is a multiple–choice format and is used to precisely placing you at the correct level of introductory classes.

The Next-Generation ACCUPLACER uses the computer–adaptive technology and the questions you see are based on your skill level. Your response to each question drives the difficulty level of the next question.

There are five sub sections on the Accuplacer test:

- Arithmetic (20 questions)
- Quantitative Reasoning, Algebra, And Statistics (QAS)(20 questions)
- Advanced Algebra and Functions (20 questions)
- Reading (20 questions)
- Writing (25 questions)

Accuplacer does NOT permit the use of personal calculators on the Math portion of placement test. Accuplacer expects students to be able to answer certain questions without the assistance of a calculator. Therefore, they provide an onscreen calculator for students to use on some questions.

Accuplacer Math Test-Taking Strategies

Here are some test-taking strategies that you can use to maximize your performance and results on the Accuplacer Math test.

#1: USE THIS APPROACH TO ANSWER EVERY ACCUPLACER MATH QUESTION

- Review the question to identify keywords and important information.

- Translate the keywords into math operations so you can solve the problem.

- Review the answer choices. What are the differences between answer choices?

- Draw or label a diagram if needed.

- Try to find patterns.

- Find the right method to answer the question. Use straightforward math, plug in numbers, or test the answer choices (backsolving).

- Double-check your work.

#2: USE EDUCATED GUESSING

This approach is applicable to the problems you understand to some degree but cannot solve using straightforward math. In such cases, try to filter out as many answer choices as possible before picking an answer. In cases where you don't have a clue about what a certain problem entails, don't waste any time trying to eliminate answer choices. Just choose one randomly before moving onto the next question.

As you can ascertain, direct solutions are the most optimal approach. Carefully read through the question, determine what the solution is using the math you have learned before, then coordinate the answer with one of the choices available to you. Are you stumped? Make your best guess, then move on.

Don't leave any fields empty! Even if you're unable to work out a problem, strive to answer it. Take a guess if you have to. You will not lose points by getting an answer wrong, though you may gain a point by getting it correct!

#3 : BALLPARK

A ballpark answer is a rough approximation. When we become overwhelmed by calculations and figures, we end up making silly mistakes. A decimal that is moved by one unit can change an answer from right to wrong, regardless of the number of steps that you went through to get it. That's where ballparking can play a big part.

If you think you know what the correct answer may be (even if it's just a ballpark answer), you'll usually have the ability to eliminate a couple of choices. While answer choices are usually based on the average student error and/or values that are closely tied, you will still be able to weed out choices that are way far afield. Try to find answers that aren't in the proverbial ballpark when you're looking for a wrong answer on a multiple-choice question. This is an optimal approach to eliminating answers to a problem.

#4 : BACKSOLVING

All questions on the Accuplacer Math test will be in multiple-choice format. Many test-takers prefer multiple-choice questions, as at least the answer is right there. You'll typically have four answers to pick from. You simply need to figure out which one is correct. Usually, the best way to go about doing so is "backsolving."

As mentioned earlier, direct solutions are the most optimal approach to answering a question. Carefully read through a problem, calculate a solution, then correspond the answer with one of the choices displayed in front of you. If you can't calculate a solution, your next best approach involves "backsolving."

When backsolving a problem, contrast one of your answer options against the problem you are asked, then see which of them is most relevant. More often than not, answer choices are listed in ascending or descending order. In such cases, try out the choices B or C. If it's not correct, you can go either down or up from there.

#5 : PLUGGING IN NUMBERS

"Plugging in numbers" is a strategy that can be applied to a wide range of different math problems on the Accuplacer Math test. This approach is typically used to simplify a challenging question so that it is more understandable. By using the strategy carefully, you can find the answer without too much trouble.

The concept is fairly straightforward–replace unknown variables in a problem with certain values. When selecting a number, consider the following:

- Choose a number that's basic (just not too basic). Generally, you should avoid choosing 1 (or even 0). A decent choice is 2.

- Try not to choose a number that is displayed in the problem.

- Make sure you keep your numbers different if you need to choose at least two of them.

- More often than not, choosing numbers merely lets you filter out some of your answer choices. As such, don't just go with the first choice that gives you the right answer.

- If several answers seem correct, then you'll need to choose another value and try again. This time, though, you'll just need to check choices that haven't been eliminated yet.

- If your question contains fractions, then a potential right answer may involve either an LCD (least common denominator) or an LCD multiple.

- 100 is the number you should choose when you are dealing with problems involving percentages.

Accuplacer Math – Test Day Tips

After practicing and reviewing all the math concepts you've been taught, and taking some Accuplacer mathematics practice tests, you'll be prepared for test day. Consider the following tips to be extra-ready come test time.

Before Your Test

What to do the night before:

- **Relax!** One day before your test, study lightly or skip studying altogether. You shouldn't attempt to learn something new, either. There are plenty of reasons why studying the evening before a big test can work against you. Put it this way–a marathoner wouldn't go out for a sprint before the day of a big race. Mental marathoners–such as yourself–should not study for any more than one hour 24 hours before a Accuplacer test. That's because your brain requires some rest to be at its best. The night before your exam, spend some time with family or friends, or read a book.

- **Avoid bright screens** - You'll have to get some good shuteye the night before your test. Bright screens (such as the ones coming from your laptop, TV, or mobile device) should be avoided altogether. Staring at such a screen will keep your brain up, making it hard to drift asleep at a reasonable hour.

- **Make sure your dinner is healthy** - The meal that you have for dinner should be nutritious. Be sure to drink plenty of water as well. Load up on your complex carbohydrates, much like a marathon runner would do. Pasta, rice, and potatoes are ideal options here, as are vegetables and protein sources.

- **Get your bag ready for test day** - The night prior to your test, pack your bag with your stationery, admissions pass, ID, and any other gear that you need. Keep the bag right by your front door.

- **Make plans to reach the testing site** - Before going to sleep, ensure that you understand precisely how you will arrive at the site of the test. If parking is something you'll have to find first, plan for it. If you're dependent on public transit, then review the schedule. You should also make sure that the train/bus/subway/streetcar you use will be running. Find out about road closures as well. If a parent or friend is accompanying you, ensure that they understand what steps they have to take as well.

The Day of the Test

- **Get up reasonably early, but not too early.**

- **Have breakfast** - Breakfast improves your concentration, memory, and mood. As such, make sure the breakfast that you eat in the morning is healthy. The last thing you want to be is distracted by a grumbling tummy. If it's not your own stomach making those noises, another test taker close to you might be instead. Prevent discomfort or embarrassment by consuming a healthy breakfast. Bring a snack with you if you think you'll need it.

- **Follow your daily routine** - Do you watch Good Morning America each morning while getting ready for the day? Don't break your usual habits on the day of the test. Likewise, if coffee isn't something you drink in the morning, then don't take up the habit hours before your test. Routine consistency lets you concentrate on the main objective–doing the best you can on your test.

- **Wear layers** - Dress yourself up in comfortable layers. You should be ready for any kind of internal temperature. If it gets too warm during the test, take a layer off.

- **Get there on time** - The last thing you want to do is get to the test site late. Rather, you should be there 45 minutes prior to the start of the test. Upon your arrival, try not to hang out with anybody who is nervous. Any anxious energy they exhibit shouldn't influence you.

- **Leave the books at home** - No books should be brought to the test site. If you start developing anxiety before the test, books could encourage you to do some last-minute studying, which will only hinder you. Keep the books far away–better yet, leave them at home.

- **Make your voice heard** - If something is off, speak to a proctor. If medical attention is needed or if you'll require anything, consult the proctor prior to the start of the test. Any doubts you have should be clarified. You should be entering the test site with a state of mind that is completely clear.

■ **Have faith in yourself** - When you feel confident, you will be able to perform at your best. When you are waiting for the test to begin, envision yourself receiving an outstanding result. Try to see yourself as someone who knows all the answers, no matter what the questions are. A lot of athletes tend to use this technique– particularly before a big competition. Your expectations will be reflected by your performance.

During your test

■ **Be calm and breathe deeply** - You need to relax before the test, and some deep breathing will go a long way to help you do that. Be confident and calm. You got this. Everybody feels a little stressed out just before an evaluation of any kind is set to begin. Learn some effective breathing exercises. Spend a minute meditating before the test starts. Filter out any negative thoughts you have. Exhibit confidence when having such thoughts.

■ **Concentrate on the test** - Refrain from comparing yourself to anyone else. You shouldn't be distracted by the people near you or random noise. Concentrate exclusively on the test. If you find yourself irritated by surrounding noises, earplugs can be used to block sounds off close to you. Don't forget–the test is going to last several hours if you're taking more than one subject of the test. Some of that time will be dedicated to brief sections. Concentrate on the specific section you are working on during a particular moment. Do not let your mind wander off to upcoming or previous sections.

■ **Try to answer each question individually** - Focus only on the question you are working on. Use one of the test-taking strategies to solve the problem. If you aren't able to come up with an answer, don't get frustrated. Simply skip that question, then move onto the next one.

■ **Don't forget to breathe!** Whenever you notice your mind wandering, your stress levels boosting, or frustration brewing, take a thirty-second break. Shut your eyes, drop your pencil, breathe deeply, and let your shoulders relax. You will end up being more productive when you allow yourself to relax for a moment.

■ **Optimize your breaks** - When break time comes, use the restroom, have a snack, and reactivate your energy for the subsequent section. Doing some stretches can help stimulate your blood flow.

After your test

■ **Take it easy** - You will need to set some time aside to relax and decompress once the test has concluded. There is no need to stress yourself out about what you could've said, or what you may have done wrong. At this point, there's nothing you can do about it. Your energy and time would be better spent on something that will bring you happiness for the remainder of your day.

■ **Redoing the test** - Did you pass the test? Congratulations! Your hard work paid off!

If you have failed your test, though, don't worry! The test can be retaken. In such cases, you will need to follow the retake policy. You also need to re-register to take the exam again.

Contents

Time to test

Time to refine your Math skill with a practice test

In this book, there are five complete Accuplacer Next Generation Mathematics Tests. Take these tests to simulate the test day experience. After you've finished, score your test using the answer keys.

Before You Start

- You'll need a pencil and a calculator to take the test.

- For each question, there are four possible answers. Choose which one is best.

- It's okay to guess. There is no penalty for wrong answers.

- After you've finished the test, review the answer key to see where you went wrong.

Good Luck!

Next Generation

Accuplacer Mathematics

Practice Test 1

2021-2022

Section 1:
Arithmetic

(No Calculator)

20 questions

Total time for this section: No time limit.

You may NOT use a calculator on this Section.

(On a real Accuplacer test, there is an onscreen calculator to use on some questions.)

1) Which of the following expression is not equal to 6?

A. $24 \times \frac{1}{4}$

B. $2 \times \frac{6}{2}$

C. $5 \times \frac{6}{5}$

D. $6 \times \frac{1}{6}$

2) What is the value of 3.56×7.8?

A. 27.768

B. 28.08

C. 277.68

D. 280.80

3) 20% of what number is equal to 85?

A. 11.25

B. 112.50

C. 200

D. 425

4) Which of the following is greater than $\frac{12}{8}$?

A. $\frac{1}{2}$

B. $\frac{5}{2}$

C. $\frac{3}{4}$

D. 1

5) A taxi driver earns $10 per 1-hour work. If he works 10 hours a day and in 1 hour he uses 2-liters petrol with price $1 for 1-liter. How much money does he earn in one day?

A. $90

B. $88

C. $80

D. $60

6) Which of the following is closest to 5.03?

A. 6

B. 5.5

C. 5

D. 5.4

7) The price of a sofa is decreased by 15% to $476. What was its original price?

A. $480

B. $520

C. $560

D. $600

8) If 40% of a class are girls, and 25% of girls play tennis, what percent of the class play tennis?

A. 10%

B. 15%

C. 20%

D. 40%

9) If 60% of A is 20% of B, then B is what percent of A?

A. 3%

B. 30%

C. 200%

D. 300%

10) The price of a car was $20,000 in 2014, $16,000 in 2015 and $12,800 in 2016. What is the rate of depreciation of the price of car per year?

A. 15%

B. 20%

C. 25%

D. 30%

11) A bank is offering 4.5% simple interest on a savings account. If you deposit $8,000, how much interest will you earn in five years?

A. $360

B. $720

C. $1,800

D. $3,600

12) Which of the following could be the value of x if $\frac{6}{8} + x > 2$?

A. $\frac{1}{3}$

B. $\frac{3}{5}$

C. $\frac{6}{5}$

D. $\frac{4}{3}$

13) 25 is what percent of 20?

A. 20%

B. 25%

C. 125%

D. 150%

14) What is the value of $2.85 + 0.045 + 0.1265$?

A. 2.2565

B. 3.0215

C. 3.215

D. 3.4265

15) How long does a 420–miles trip take moving at 50 miles per hour (mph)?

A. 4 $hours$

B. 6 $hours$ and 24 $minutes$

C. 8 $hours$ and 24 $minutes$

D. 8 $hours$ and 30 $minutes$

16) Which of the following lists shows the fractions in order from least to greatest?

$$\frac{3}{4}, \frac{2}{7}, \frac{3}{8}, \frac{5}{11}$$

A. $\frac{3}{8}, \frac{2}{7}, \frac{3}{4}, \frac{5}{11}$

B. $\frac{2}{7}, \frac{5}{11}, \frac{3}{8}, \frac{3}{4}$

C. $\frac{2}{7}, \frac{3}{8}, \frac{5}{11}, \frac{3}{4}$

D. $\frac{3}{8}, \frac{2}{7}, \frac{5}{11}, \frac{3}{4}$

17) $\frac{4}{5} - \frac{3}{5} = ?$

A. 0.35

B. 0.3

C. 0.2

D. 0.025

18) Sophia purchased a sofa for $530.40 The sofa is regularly priced at $624 What was the percent discount Sophia received on the sofa?

A. 12%

B. 15%

C. 20%

D. 25%

19) A rope weighs 600 grams per meter of length. What is the weight in kilograms of 12.2 meters of this rope? ($1 \ kilograms = 1,000 \ grams$)

A. 0.0732

B. 0.732

C. 7.32

D. 73.20

20) When number 91,501 is divided by 305, the result is closest to?

A. 3

B. 30

C. 300

D. 350

STOP: This is the End of Section 1 of test 1.

Next Generation

Accuplacer Mathematics

Practice Test 1

2021-2022

Section 2:

Quantitative Reasoning, Algebra, and Statistics

(No Calculator)

20 questions

Total time for this section: No time limit.

You may NOT use a calculator on this Section.

(On a real Accuplacer test, there is an onscreen calculator to use on some questions.)

6

1) When a number is subtracted from 24 and the difference is divided by that number, the result is 3. What is the value of the number?

A. 2

B. 4

C. 6

D. 12

2) An angle is equal to one ninth of its supplement. What is the measure of that angle?

A. 18

B. 24

C. 36

D. 45

3) John traveled 150 km in 6 hours and Alice traveled 180 km in 4 hours. What is the ratio of the average speed of John to average speed of Alice?

A. 3 : 2

B. 2 : 3

C. 5 : 9

D. 5 : 6

4) If $\frac{30}{A} + 1 = 7$, then $30 + A = ?$

A. 2

B. 7

C. 35

D. 40

5) Right triangle ABC has two legs of lengths 9 cm (AB) and 12 cm (AC). What is the length of the third side (BC)?

A. 6 cm

B. 8 cm

C. 14 cm

D. 15 cm

6) The area of a circle is less than 64π. Which of the following can be the circumference of the circle?

A. 12π

B. 16π

C. 24π

D. 32π

7) The width of a box is one third of its length. The height of the box is one third of its width. If the length of the box is $27cm$, what is the volume of the box?

A. $81\ cm^3$

B. $162\ cm^3$

C. $243\ cm^3$

D. $729\ cm^3$

8) How many possible outfit combinations come from six shirts, three slacks, and five ties?

A. 15

B. 18

C. 30

D. 90

9) If the area of the following rectangular $ABCD$ is 100, and E is the midpoint of AB, what is the area of the shaded part

A. 25

B. 45

C. 50

D. 100

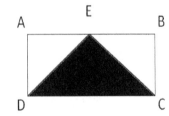

10) What is the slope of a line that is perpendicular to the line $2x - 4y = 24$?

A. -2

B. 2

C. $-\frac{1}{2}$

D. $\frac{1}{2}$

11) Two third of 18 is equal to $\frac{2}{5}$ of what number?

A. 12

B. 20

C. 30

D. 60

12) A boat sails 40 miles south and then 30 miles east. How far is the boat from its start point?

A. 45 *miles*

B. 50 *miles*

C. 60 *miles*

D. 70 *miles*

13) The ratio of boys and girls in a class is $4:7$. If there are 44 students in the class, how many more boys should be enrolled to make the ratio $1:1$?

A. 8

B. 10

C. 12

D. 16

14) The score of Emma was half as that of Ava and the score of Mia was twice that of Ava. If the score of Mia was 60, what is the score of Emma?

A. 12

B. 15

C. 20

D. 30

15) A bag contains 18 balls: two green, five black, eight blue, a brown, a red and one white. If 17 balls are removed from the bag at random, what is the probability that a brown ball has been removed?

A. $\frac{1}{9}$

B. $\frac{1}{6}$

C. $\frac{16}{17}$

D. $\frac{17}{18}$

16) The average of five consecutive numbers is 38. What is the smallest number?

A. 38

B. 36

C. 34

D. 12

17) The average weight of 18 girls in a class is 60 kg and the average weight of 32 boys in the same class is 62 kg. What is the average weight of all the 50 students in that class?

A. 60

B. 61.28

C. 61.68

D. 62.90

18) What is the median of these numbers? 4, 9, 13, 8, 15, 18, 5

A. 8

B. 9

C. 13

D. 15

19) To paint a wall with the area of 57 m^2, how many liters of paint do we need if each liter of paint is enough to paint a wall with dimension of 80 $cm \times 95\ cm$?

A. 50

B. 75

C. 100

D. 150

20) In 1999, the average worker's income increased $2,000 per year starting from $24,000 annual salary. Which equation represents income greater than average? (I = income, x = number of years after 1999)

A. $I > 2000\ x + 24000$

B. $I > -2000\ x + 24000$

C. $I < -2000\ x + 24000$

D. $I < 2000\ x - 24000$

STOP: This is the End of Section 2 of test 1.

Next Generation

Accuplacer Mathematics

Practice Test 1

2021-2022

Section 3:
Advanced Algebra and Functions
(Calculator)

20 questions

Total time for this section: No time limit.

You may use a calculator on this Section.

(On a real Accuplacer test, there is an onscreen calculator to use on some questions.)

11

1) If $2x + 2y = 2$ and $3x - y = 7$, which of the following ordered pairs (x, y) satisfies both equations?

A. $(1, 3)$

B. $(2, 4)$

C. $(2, -1)$

D. $(4, -6)$

2) If $f(x) = 3x + 4(x + 1) + 2$, then $f(4x) = ?$

A. $28x + 6$

B. $16x - 6$

C. $25x + 4$

D. $12x + 3$

3) A line in the xy-plane passes through origin and has a slope of $\frac{1}{3}$. Which of the following points lies on the line?

A. $(2, 1)$

B. $(4, 1)$

C. $(9, 3)$

D. $(6, 3)$

4) Which of the following is equivalent to $(3n^2 + 2n + 6) - (2n^2 - 4)$?

A. $n + 4n^2$

B. $n^2 - 3$

C. $n^2 + 2n + 10$

D. $n + 2$

5) Solve for x: $4(x + 1) = 6(x - 4) + 20$

A. 12

B. 6.5

C. 4

D. 2

6) If $x \neq -4$ and $x \neq 5$, which of the following is equivalent to $\dfrac{1}{\frac{1}{x-5}+\frac{1}{x+4}}$?

A. $\dfrac{(x-5)(x+4)}{(x-5)+(x+4)}$

B. $\dfrac{(x+4)+(x-5)}{(x+4)(x-5)}$

C. $\dfrac{(x+4)(x-5)}{(x+4)-(x+5)}$

D. $\dfrac{(x+4)+(x-5)}{(x+4)-(x-5)}$

$$y < c - x \,, y > x + b$$

7) In the xy-plane, if $(0,0)$ is a solution to the system of inequalities above, which of the following relationships between c and b must be true?

A. $c < b$

B. $c > b$

C. $c = b$

D. $c = b + c$

8) What is the value of x in the following equation? $3x + 10 = 46$

A. 4

B. 7

C. 10

D. 12

9) Calculate $f(5)$ for the following function.

$$f(x) = x^2 - 3x$$

A. 5

B. 10

C. 15

D. 20

10) John buys a pepper plant that is 5 inches tall. With regular watering the plant grows 3 inches a year. Writing John's plant's height as a function of time, what does the y −intercept represent?

A. The y −intercept represents the rate of grows of the plant which is 5 inches

B. The y −intercept represents the starting height of 5 inches

C. The y −intercept represents the rate of growth of plant which is 3 inches per year

D. There is no y −intercept

11) If $\frac{4}{x} = \frac{12}{x-8}$ what is the value of $\frac{x}{2}$?

A. 1

B. 3

C. −2

D. 2

12) Which of the following is an equation of a circle in the xy-plane with center $(-1, 2)$ and a radius with endpoint $(2, 6)$?

A. $(x + 1)^2 + (y - 2)^2 = 5$

B. $2x^2 + (y + 2)^2 = 25$

C. $(x - 1)^2 + (y - 2)^2 = 5$

D. $(x + 1)^2 + (y - 2)^2 = 25$

13) Given a right triangle ΔABC whose $\angle B = 90°, sin\ C = \frac{8}{17}$, find $\cos A$?

A. 1

B. $\frac{8}{15}$

C. $\frac{8}{17}$

D. $\frac{15}{17}$

14) The circle graph below shows all Mr. Green's expenses for last month. If he spent $660 on his car, how much did he spend for his rent?

A. $700

B. $740

C. $810

D. $910

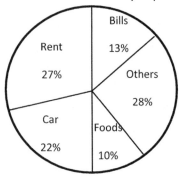

Mr. Green's monthly expenses

15) The Jackson Library is ordering some bookshelves. If x is the number of bookshelves the library wants to order, which each cost $200 and there is a one-time delivery charge of $600, which of the following represents the total cost, in dollar, per bookshelf?

A. $\dfrac{200x+600}{x}$

B. $\dfrac{200x+600}{200}$

C. $200 + 600x$

D. $200x + 600$

16) A function $g(3) = 5$ and $g(5) = 4$. A function $f(5) = 2$ and $f(4) = 6$. What is the value of $f(g(5))$?

A. 5

B. 6

C. 7

D. 8

17) What is the area of the following equilateral triangle if the side $AB = 12\ cm$?

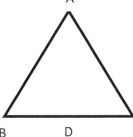

A. $36\sqrt{3}\ cm^2$

B. $18\sqrt{3}\ cm^2$

C. $6\sqrt{3}\ cm^2$

D. $8\ cm^2$

18) If $x \blacksquare y = \sqrt{x^2 + y}$, what is the value of $6\blacksquare28$?

A. $\sqrt{168}$

B. 10

C. 8

D. 6

$$x^2 + y^2 + 8x - 2y = 1$$

19) The equation of a circle in the $xy-$plane is shown above. What is the radius of the circle?

A. 24

B. 18

C. $3\sqrt{2}$

D. $\sqrt{10}$

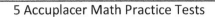

20) What is the value of x in the following figure? (Figure is not drawn to scale)

A. 150

B. 145

C. 125

D. 105

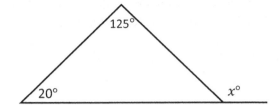

STOP: This is the End of Test 1.

Next Generation

Accuplacer Mathematics

Practice Test 2

2021-2022

Section 1:
Arithmetic
(No Calculator)

20 questions

Total time for this section: No time limit.

You may NOT use a calculator on this Section.

(On a real Accuplacer test, there is an onscreen calculator to use on some questions.)

1) What is 5 percent of 480?

A. 20

B. 24

C. 30

D. 40

2) In two successive years, the population of a town is increased by 15% and 20%. What percent of the population is increased after two years?

A. 32%

B. 35%

C. 38%

D. 68%

3) For what price is 15 percent off the same as $75 off?

A. $200

B. $300

C. $350

D. $500

4) Last week 24,000 fans attended a football match. This week three times as many bought tickets, but one sixth of them cancelled their tickets. How many are attending this week?

A. 48,000

B. 54,000

C. 60,000

D. 72,000

5) Which of the following shows the numbers in increasing order?

$$\frac{2}{3}, 0.68, 67\%, \frac{4}{5}$$

A. $67\%, 0.68, \frac{2}{3}, \frac{4}{5}$

B. $67\%, 0.68, \frac{4}{5}, \frac{2}{3}$

C. $0.68, 67\%, \frac{2}{3}, \frac{4}{5}$

D. $\frac{2}{3}, 67\%, 0.68, \frac{4}{5}$

6) What is $12,181 + 8,591$?

A. 20,772

B. 20,872

C. 21,776

D. 22,771

7) Bob deposits 15% of $160 into a savings account, what is the amount of his deposit?

A. $10

B. $16

C. $20

D. $24

8) If 150% of a number is 75, then what is the 90% of that number?

A. 45

B. 50

C. 70

D. 85

9) What is the remainder when 1,454 is divided by 7?

A. 2

B. 3

C. 5

D. 6

10) Which of the following numbers is less than $\frac{3}{2}$?

A. 1.4

B. $\frac{5}{2}$

C. 3

D. 2.8

11) Mr. Jones saves $2,500 out of his monthly family income of $55,000. What fractional part of his income does he save?

A. $\frac{1}{22}$

B. $\frac{1}{11}$

C. $\frac{3}{25}$

D. $\frac{2}{15}$

12) 16% of what number is equal to 72?

A. 8.64

B. 36

C. 300

D. 450

13) 55 students took an exam and 11 of them failed. What percent of the students passed the exam?

A. 20%

B. 40%

C. 60%

D. 80%

14) If $\frac{6}{5} \div \frac{1}{8} = x$, then the value of x is between which of the following pairs of numbers?

A. 4 and 6

B. 8 and 10

C. 12 and 15

D. 15 and 20

15) What is 0.5749 rounded to the nearest hundredth?

A. 0.57

B. 0.575

C. 0.58

D. 0.584

16) If a gas tank can hold 28 gallons, how many gallons does it contain when it is $\frac{3}{4}$ full?

A. 14 gallons

B. 16 gallons

C. 19 gallons

D. 21 gallons

17) Ethan needs an 75% average in his writing class to pass. On his first 4 exams, he earned scores of 68%, 72%, 85%, and 90%. What is the minimum score Ethan can earn on his fifth and final test to pass?

A. 80%

B. 70%

C. 68%

D. 60%

18) What is 120.756 rounded to the nearest hundredth?

A. 120

B. 120.75

C. 120.76

D. 121

$$\frac{5}{8}, 0.625\%, 0.0625$$

19) Which of the following correctly orders the values above from greatest to least?

A. $0.625\%, \frac{5}{8}, 0.0625$

B. $0.0625, 0.625\%, \frac{5}{8}$

C. $\frac{5}{8}, 0.625\%, 0.0625$

D. $\frac{5}{8}, 0.0625, 0.625\%$

20) Which of the following is equivalent to $\frac{2}{5}$?

A. 0.04

B. 0.25

C. 0.40

D. 1.4

STOP: This is the End of Section 1 of test 2.

Next Generation

Accuplacer Mathematics

Practice Test 2

2021-2022

Section 2:

Quantitative Reasoning, Algebra, And Statistics

(No Calculator)

20 questions

Total time for this section: No time limit.

You may NOT use a calculator on this Section.

(On a real Accuplacer test, there is an onscreen calculator to use on some questions.)

1) In a stadium the ratio of home fans to visiting fans in a crowd is 5: 7. Which of the following could be the total number of fans in the stadium?

A. 12,324

B. 42,326

C. 44,566

D. 66,812

2) Which of the following points lies on the line $2x - y = -6$?

A. $(-1, 4)$

B. $(2, 2)$

C. $(1, 3)$

D. $(3, 1)$

3) Which graph shows a non-proportional linear relationship between x and y?

A.

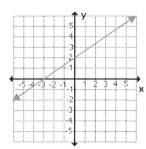

B.

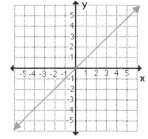

C.

D.

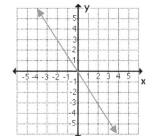

4) The mean of 50 test scores was calculated as 88. But it turned out that one of the scores was misread as 94 but it was 69. What is the correct mean of the test scores?

A. 85

B. 87

C. 87.5

D. 88.5

5) Two dice are thrown simultaneously, what is the probability of getting a sum of 6 or 9?

A. $\frac{1}{3}$

B. $\frac{1}{4}$

C. $\frac{1}{6}$

D. $\frac{1}{12}$

6) A swimming pool holds 2,000 cubic feet of water. The swimming pool is 25 feet long and 10 feet wide. How deep is the swimming pool?

A. 2

B. 4

C. 6

D. 8

7) What is the area of a square whose diagonal is 8?

A. 16

B. 32

C. 36

D. 64

8) Anita's trick–or–treat bag contains 12 pieces of chocolate, 18 suckers, 18 pieces of gum, 24 pieces of licorice. If she randomly pulls a piece of candy from her bag, what is the probability of her pulling out a piece of sucker?

A. $\frac{1}{3}$

B. $\frac{1}{4}$

C. $\frac{1}{6}$

D. $\frac{1}{12}$

9) The average of 6 numbers is 12. The average of 4 of those numbers is 10. What is the average of the other two numbers?

A. 10

B. 12

C. 14

D. 16

10) The perimeter of the trapezoid below is 36 cm. What is its area?

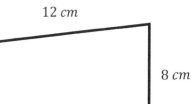

A. 576 cm^2

B. 70 cm^2

C. 48 cm^2

D. 24 cm^2

11) A football team had $20,000 to spend on supplies. The team spent $14,000 on new balls. New sport shoes cost $120 each. Which of the following inequalities represent the number of new shoes the team can purchase?

A. $120x + 14,000 \leq 20,000$

B. $120x + 14,000 \geq 20,000$

C. $14,000x + 120 \leq 20,000$

D. $14,000x + 120 \geq 20,000$

12) A card is drawn at random from a standard 52–card deck, what is the probability that the card is of Hearts? (The deck includes 13 of each suit clubs, diamonds, hearts, and spades)

A. $\frac{1}{3}$

B. $\frac{1}{4}$

C. $\frac{1}{6}$

D. $\frac{1}{52}$

13) The average of five numbers is 24. If a sixth number that is greater than 42 is added, then, which of the following could be the new average? (Select one or more answer choices)

A. 25

B. 26

C. 27

D. 28

14) The length of a rectangle is 3 times of its width. If the length is 24, what is the perimeter of the rectangle

A. 74

B. 64

C. 36

D. 48

15) The ratio of oranges and apples in a basket is $3:8$. If there are 55 fruits in the basket, how many apples are in the basket?

A. 6

B. 25

C. 35

D. 40

16) What is the value of x in the following equation?

$$\frac{2}{3}x + \frac{1}{6} = \frac{1}{3}$$

A. 6

B. $\frac{1}{2}$

C. $\frac{1}{3}$

D. $\frac{1}{4}$

17) If $y = 2b^2 + 3ab + 3a^3$, what is y when $a = 3$ and $b = 2$?

A. 53

B. 103

C. 107

D. 116

18) Right triangle ABC has two legs of lengths 5 cm (AB) and 12 cm (AC). What is the length of the third side (BC)?

A. 4 cm

B. 6 cm

C. 8 cm

D. 13 cm

19) If $\frac{4x}{18} = \frac{x+1}{9}$, $x =$?

A. 2

B. 1

C. −1

D. −2

20) Simplify. $\dfrac{\frac{1}{3} - \frac{x+6}{6}}{\frac{x^2}{2} - \frac{4}{2}}$

A. $\frac{-2x-4}{6x^2-24}$

B. $\frac{2x+8}{6x^2-24}$

C. $\frac{x+4}{3x^2-12}$

D. $\frac{-x-4}{3x^2-12}$

STOP: This is the End of Section 2 of test 2.

Next Generation

Accuplacer Mathematics

Practice Test 2

2021-2022

Section 3:

Advanced Algebra and Functions

(Calculator)

20 questions

Total time for this section: No time limit.

You may use a calculator on this Section.

(On a real Accuplacer test, there is an onscreen calculator to use on some questions.)

28

1) If $\frac{x-3}{5} = N$ and $N = 6$, what is the value of x?

A. 25

B. 28

C. 30

D. 33

2) Which of the following is equal to $b^{\frac{3}{5}}$?

A. $\sqrt[3]{b^{\frac{5}{3}}}$

B. $b^{\frac{5}{3}}$

C. $\sqrt[5]{b^3}$

D. $\sqrt[3]{b^5}$

3) On Saturday, Sara read N pages of a book each hour for 3 hours, and Mary read M pages of a book each hour for 4 hours. Which of the following represents the total number of pages of book read by Sara and Mary on Saturday?

A. $12MN$

B. $3N + 4M$

C. $7MN$

D. $4N + 3M$

4) Simplify $(-4 + 9i)(3 + 5i)$.

A. $54 - 7i$

B. $-54 + 7i$

C. $-57 + 7i$

D. $57 - 7i$

5) If function is defined as $f(x) = bx^2 + 15$, and b is a constant and $f(2) = 35$. What is the value of $f(5)$?

A. 25

B. 35

C. 140

D. 165

6) Find the solution (x, y) to the following system of equations?

$$2x + 5y = 11$$
$$4x - 2y = -14$$

A. $(14, 5)$

B. $(6, 8)$

C. $(11, 17)$

D. $(-2, 3)$

7) Calculate $f(4)$ for the function $f(x) = 3x^2 - 4$.

A. 44

B. 40

C. 38

D. 30

8) What are the zeroes of the function $f(x) = x^3 + 5x^2 + 6x$?

A. 0

B. 2

C. $0, 2, 3$

D. $0, -2, -3$

9) Simplify $\frac{4-3i}{-4i}$?

A. i

B. $\frac{3i}{4}$

C. $\frac{3}{4} - i$

D. $\frac{3}{4} + i$

$$y = x^2 - 7x + 12$$

10) The equation above represents a parabola in the xy-plane. Which of the following equivalent forms of the equation displays the x-intercepts of the parabola as constants or coefficients?

A. $y = x + 3$

B. $y = x(x - 7)$

C. $y = (x + 3)(x + 4)$

D. $y = (x - 3)(x - 4)$

11) The function $g(x)$ is defined by a polynomial. Some values of x and $g(x)$ are shown in the table below. Which of the following must be a factor of $g(x)$?

A. x

B. $x - 1$

C. $x - 2$

D. $x + 1$

x	$g(x)$
0	5
1	4
2	0

12) What is the value of $\dfrac{4b}{c}$ when $\dfrac{c}{b} = 2$

A. 8

B. 4

C. 2

D. 1

13) If $x + 5 = 8$, $2y - 1 = 5$ then $xy + 15 =$

A. 30

B. 24

C. 21

D. 17

14) If $\dfrac{a-b}{b} = \dfrac{10}{13}$, then which of the following must be true?

A. $\dfrac{a}{b} = \dfrac{10}{13}$

B. $\dfrac{a}{b} = \dfrac{23}{13}$

C. $\dfrac{a}{b} = \dfrac{13}{21}$

D. $\dfrac{a}{b} = \dfrac{21}{10}$

15) Which of the following lines is parallel to: $6y - 2x = 24$

A. $y = \dfrac{1}{3}x + 4$

B. $y = 3x + 5$

C. $y = x - 2$

D. $y = 2x - 1$

16) The average of $13, 15, 20$ and x is 20. What is the value of x

A. 9

B. 15

C. 18

D. 32

17) Find the value of x in the following diagram?

A. 25

B. 33

C. 35

D. 47

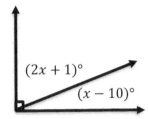

18) If the interior angles of a quadrilateral are in the ratio $1: 2: 3: 4$, what is the measure of the smallest angle?

A. $36°$

B. $72°$

C. $108°$

D. $144°$

19) Sara orders a box of pen for $3 per box. A tax of 8.5% is added to the cost of the pens before a flat shipping fee of $6 closest out the transaction. Which of the following represents total cost of p boxes of pens in dollars?

A. $1.085(3p) + 6$

B. $6p + 3$

C. $1.085(6p) + 3$

D. $3p + 6$

20) A plant grows at a linear rate. After five weeks, the plant is $40\ cm$ tall. Which of the following functions represents the relationship between the height (y) of the plant and number of weeks of growth (x)?

A. $y(x) = 40x + 8$

B. $y(x) = 8x + 40$

C. $y(x) = 40x$

D. $y(x) = 8x$

STOP: This is the End of Test 2.

Next Generation

Accuplacer Mathematics

Practice Test 3

2021-2022

Section 1:
Arithmetic

(No Calculator)

20 questions

Total time for this section: No time limit.

You may NOT use a calculator on this Section.

(On a real Accuplacer test, there is an onscreen calculator to use on some questions.)

1) Which of the following inequalities is true?

A. $\frac{3}{4} < \frac{17}{24}$

B. $\frac{2}{3} < \frac{5}{9}$

C. $\frac{3}{8} < \frac{9}{25}$

D. $\frac{11}{21} < \frac{4}{7}$

2) What is the value of 4.56×7.8?

A. 35.568

B. 36.08

C. 355.68

D. 360.80

3) 12% of what number is equal to 72?

A. 11.25

B. 112.50

C. 400

D. 600

4) Which of the following is greater than $\frac{13}{8}$?

A. $\frac{1}{2}$

B. $\frac{5}{2}$

C. $\frac{3}{4}$

D. 1

5) What is the remainder when 879 is divided by 9?

A. 0

B. 3

C. 5

D. 6

6) What is the value of $0.0001 \times 2,782.5$?

A. 27.825

B. 2.7825

C. 0.27825

D. 0.027825

7) What is 2.5% of 650 ?

A. $\frac{13}{8}$

B. $\frac{13}{80}$

C. $\frac{65}{2}$

D. $\frac{65}{4}$

8) What is the value of $\frac{6}{20} + \frac{1}{80}$?

A. $\frac{5}{16}$

B. $\frac{7}{16}$

C. $\frac{7}{40}$

D. $\frac{7}{20}$

9) If $\frac{6}{3} \div \frac{1}{4} = n$, then the value of n is between which of the following pairs of numbers?

A. 3 and 4

B. 4 and 5

C. 6 and 8

D. 7 and 9

10) In March, an athlete weighed 200 pounds. In November, the same athlete weighed 165 pounds. What is the athlete's percentage of weight loss?

A. 15%

B. 17.50%

C. 25%

D. 32.50%

11) $-4(8 \div 2)^2 =?$

A. -8

B. -16

C. -64

D. -240

12) Which of the following expressions has the same value as $\frac{5}{4} \times \frac{6}{2}$?

A. $\frac{6 \times 3}{4}$

B. $\frac{6 \times 2}{4}$

C. $\frac{5 \times 6}{4}$

D. $\frac{5 \times 3}{4}$

13) 35 is What percent of 20?

A. 20%

B. 25%

C. 175%

D. 190%

14) What is the value of $3.85 + 0.045 + 0.1365$?

A. 2.2565

B. 4.0315

C. 4.215

D. 4.4265

15) $(-2)^3 + (-4)^2 =?$

A. -24

B. 24

C. 8

D. -8

16) Which of the following lists shows the fractions in order from greatest to least?

$$\frac{2}{3}, \frac{7}{8}, \frac{9}{11}, \frac{3}{5}$$

A. $\frac{9}{11}, \frac{7}{8}, \frac{2}{3}, \frac{3}{5}$

B. $\frac{7}{8}, \frac{9}{11}, \frac{2}{3}, \frac{3}{5}$

C. $\frac{7}{8}, \frac{2}{3}, \frac{9}{11}, \frac{3}{5}$

D. $\frac{3}{5}, \frac{7}{8}, \frac{2}{3}, \frac{9}{11}$

17) $\frac{2}{4} + \frac{3}{2} - \frac{1}{4} = ?$

A. 0.75

B. 1.5

C. 1.75

D. 2.25

18) $\frac{(8+6)^2}{2} + 6 = ?$

A. 110

B. 104

C. 90

D. 14

19) An 80 pound coil of cable is 400 feet long. If a 20 foot length is cut off, what is the weight in pounds of the remaining cable?

A. 70

B. 73

C. 76

D. 81

20) When 78 is divided by 5, the remainder is the same as when 45 is divided by

A. 2

B. 4

C. 5

D. 7

STOP: This is the End of Section1 of test 3.

Next Generation

Accuplacer Mathematics

Practice Test 3

2021-2022

Section 2:
Quantitative Reasoning, Algebra, And Statistics

(No Calculator)

20 questions

Total time for this section: No time limit.

You may NOT use a calculator on this Section.

(On a real Accuplacer test, there is an onscreen calculator to use on some questions.)

1) Simplify this expression. $\dfrac{(-2x^2y^2)^3(3x^3y)}{12x^3y^8}$

A. $\dfrac{-6x^6y^7}{2y}$

B. $\dfrac{-3x^6}{2y}$

C. $\dfrac{-2x^6}{y}$

D. $\dfrac{12x^6}{y^8}$

2) Solve and write the solution set in set-builder notation of the following inequality.
$2x - 4(x + 2) \geq x + 6$

A. $\left\{x\middle|x \geq \dfrac{-14}{3}\right\}$

B. $\left\{x\middle|x \leq \dfrac{2}{3}\right\}$

C. $\left\{x\middle|x \geq \dfrac{2}{3}\right\}$

D. $\left\{x\middle|x \leq \dfrac{-14}{3}\right\}$

3) Which of the following values is equivalent to 4^{-3}?

A. $\dfrac{1}{16}$

B. -16

C. $\dfrac{1}{64}$

D. -64

4) Find the factors of the binomial $x^3 - 8$

A. $(x + 2)(x - 2)$

B. $(x^2 + 4)(x^2 - 4)$

C. $(x^2 + 2x + 4)(x - 2)$

D. $(x^2 + 2x + 4)(x + 2)$

5) Function g is defined by $g(x) = 5(x - 6)$. What is the value of $g(15)$?

A. -9

B. $+9$

C. 45

D. 69

6) If the area of a circle is 49 square meters, what is its radius?

A. $\frac{7\sqrt{\pi}}{\pi}$ m

B. $\frac{7\sqrt{\pi}}{2}$ m

C. $\frac{7\pi}{4}$ m

D. $\frac{49\sqrt{\pi}}{4}$ m

7) Solve $N = s + (a - 1)d$ for a.

A. $a = N - 1 - ad$

B. $a = \frac{N+s+d}{d}$

C. $a = \frac{Nsd}{d}$

D. $a = \frac{N-s+d}{d}$

8) A ladder leans against a wall forming a $60°$ angle between the ground and the ladder. If the bottom of the ladder is 35 feet away from the wall, how long is the ladder?

A. $40\ ft$

B. $65\ ft$

C. $70\ ft$

D. $85\ ft$

9) What is the perimeter of the following trapezoid?

A. $12\ cm$

B. $15\ cm$

C. $28\ cm$

D. $38\ cm$

10) In the xy-plane, the point $(4, 3)$ and $(3, 2)$ are on line A. Which of the following points could also be on line A?

A. $(-1, 2)$

B. $(5, 7)$

C. $(3, 4)$

D. $(-1, -2)$

11) Three fifths of 20 is equal to $\frac{3}{4}$ of what number?

A. 9

B. 12

C. 16

D. 50

12) If $f = 3x + 2y$ and $g = x - 5y$, what is $3f + g$?

A. $4x - 3y$

B. $10x + y$

C. $15x - 6y$

D. $10x - 11y$

13) The ratio of the speed of train A to the speed of train B is 6 to 5. If train B travels $500\ km$ in 5 hours, then the speed of train A is …

A. $83.4\ km/h$

B. $112\ km/h$

C. $120\ km/h$

D. $135\ km/h$

14) Three friends play the game with each other. In the dart game, the score by David was half as that of Robert and the score of James was triple that of Robert. If the score of James was 90, what is the score of David?

A. 5

B. 15

C. 20

D. 30

15) A construction company is building a wall. The company can build $40\ cm$ of the wall per minute. After 50 minutes construction, $\frac{2}{3}$ of the wall is completed. How high is the wall?

A. $10\ m$

B. $15\ m$

C. $30\ m$

D. $35\ m$

16) Which of the following represent the graph of the line with the following equation?
$$4x + 2y = 8$$

A.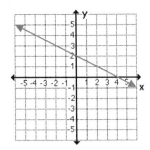

B.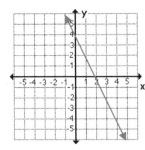

C.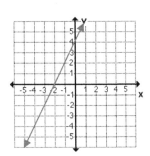

D.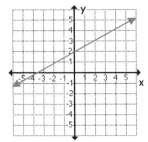

17) For his Physics class, Robert has scored 89, 76, and 98 on three of his tests so far. What is the minimum score Robert needs to receive on his 4ᵗʰ test to have an average of 90?

A. 95

B. 97

C. 98

D. 100

18) What is the median of these numbers? $3, 10, 12, 8, 15, 19, 5, 2$

A. 8

B. 9

C. 10

D. 15

19) The surface area of a cylinder is $150\pi\ cm^2$. If its height is $10\ cm$, what is the radius of the cylinder?

A. $13\ cm$

B. $11\ cm$

C. $15\ cm$

D. $5\ cm$

20) James had $80 in lunch money for school. Every day he spends $4.5 for food and drinks. What is the expression that shows how much money will he have after each day, where D is the days, and T is the total amount of money left?

A. $T = 80 - 4.5D$

B. $T = 80 + 4.5D$

C. $D = 80 - 4.5T$

D. $80 - T - 4.5D = 0$

STOP: This is the End of Section 2 of test 3.

Next Generation

Accuplacer Mathematics

Practice Test 3

2021-2022

Section 3:
Advanced Algebra and Functions
(Calculator)

20 questions

Total time for this section: No time limit.

You may use a calculator on this Section.

(On a real Accuplacer test, there is an onscreen calculator to use on some questions.)

44

1) If $x + y = 0, 4x - 2y = 24$, which of the following ordered pairs (x, y) satisfies both equations?

A. $(4, 3)$

B. $(5, 4)$

C. $(4, -4)$

D. $(4, -6)$

2) If $f(x) = 3x + 4(x + 1) + 2$ then $f(3x) = ?$

A. $21x + 6$

B. $16x - 6$

C. $25x + 4$

D. $12x + 3$

3) $(5x - 3y)^2$:

A. $25x^2 - 9y^2$

B. $25x^2 + 9y^2$

C. $25x^2 + 9y^2 - 15xy$

D. $25x^2 + 9y^2 - 30xy$

4) Which of the following is equivalent to $(3n^2 + 4n + 6) - (2n^2 - 5)$?

A. $n + 4n^2$

B. $n^2 - 3$

C. $n^2 + 4n + 11$

D. $n + 2$

5) If $(ax + 4)(bx + 3) = 10x^2 + cx + 12$ for all values of x and $a + b = 7$, what are the two possible values for c?

A. $22, 21$

B. $20, 22$

C. $23, 26$

D. $24, 23$

6) If $x \neq -4$ and $x \neq 6$, which of the following is equivalent to $\dfrac{1}{\dfrac{1}{x-6}+\dfrac{1}{x+4}}$?

A. $\dfrac{(x-6)(x+4)}{(x-6)+(x+4)}$

B. $\dfrac{(x+4)+(x-6)}{(x+4)(x-6)}$

C. $\dfrac{(x+4)(x-6)}{(x+4)-(x+6)}$

D. $\dfrac{(x+4)+(x-6)}{(x+4)-(x-6)}$

7) Which of the following best describes the range of $y = -3x^4 + 6$?

A. $y \leq -3$

B. $y \geq 6$

C. $y \leq 6$

D. All real numbers

8) Which of the following points lies on the line that goes through the points $(2, 4)$ and $(4, 5)$?

A. $(9, 9)$

B. $(9, 6)$

C. $(6, 9)$

D. $(6, 6)$

9) Calculate $f(4)$ for the following function $f(x)$.

$$f(x) = x^2 - 3x$$

A. 0

B. 4

C. 12

D. 20

10) Which lines have a $y-$intercept at $(0, 4)$?

A. $y = -3x + 5$

B. $y = 4x + 7$

C. $y = 5 + 4x$

D. $y = 4 - x$

11) If $\frac{3}{x} = \frac{12}{x-9}$ what is the value of $\frac{x}{6}$?

A. -2

B. 2

C. $-\frac{1}{2}$

D. $\frac{1}{2}$

12) Which of the following is an equation of a circle in the xy-plane with center $(0,4)$ and a radius with endpoint $(\frac{5}{3}, 6)$?

A. $(x+1)^2 + (y-4)^2 = \frac{61}{9}$

B. $2x^2 + (y+4)^2 = \frac{61}{9}$

C. $(x-2)^2 + (y-4)^2 = \frac{61}{9}$

D. $x^2 + (y-4)^2 = \frac{61}{9}$

13) Given a right triangle ΔABC whose $n\angle B = 90°$, $\sin C = \frac{2}{3}$, find $\cos A$?

A. 1

B. $\frac{1}{2}$

C. $\frac{2}{3}$

D. $\frac{3}{2}$

14) What is the equation of the following graph?

A. $y = |x| - 1$

B. $y = |x| + 1$

C. $y = -|x| + 1$

D. $y = |x + 1|$

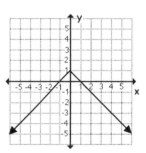

15) In the $xy-$plane, the line determined by the points $(6, m)$ and $(m, 12)$ passes through the origin. Which of the following could be the value of m?

A. $\pm\sqrt{6}$

B. ±12

C. $\pm6\sqrt{2}$

D. ±9

16) A function $g(3) = 5$ and $g(6) = 4$. A function $f(5) = 2$ and $f(4) = 7$. What is the value of $f(g(6))$?

A. 5

B. 7

C. 8

D. 9

17) The area of the following equilateral triangle with sides of length d is ...

A. $\frac{\sqrt{3}\,d^2}{4}$

B. $\frac{d^2}{4}$

C. $\frac{d^2}{2}$

D. $\frac{\sqrt{2}\,d^2}{4}$

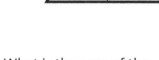

18) A circle is inscribed in a square and the radius of the circle is 4. What is the area of the shaded region?

A. $16 - 4\pi$

B. $64 - 16\pi$

C. $16 - 64\pi$

D. 16π

$$(x + 2)^2 + (y - 4)^2 = 16$$

19) In the standard (x, y) coordinate system plane, what is the area of the circle with the above equation?

A. 24π

B. 18π

C. 16π

D. $\sqrt{10}$

20) Right triangle ABC is shown below. Which of the following is true for all possible values of angle A and B?

A. $tanA = tanB$

B. $sinA = cosB$

C. $tan^2A = tan^2B$

D. $tanA = 1$

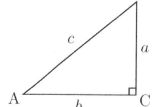

STOP: This is the End of Test 3.

Next Generation

Accuplacer Mathematics

Practice Test 4

2021-2022

Section 1:
Arithmetic

(No Calculator)

20 questions

Total time for this section: No time limit.

You may NOT use a calculator on this Section.

(On a real Accuplacer test, there is an onscreen calculator to use on some questions.)

1) What is 5 percent of 560?

A. 20

B. 28

C. 30

D. 40

2) Which of the following inequalities is true?

A. $\frac{3}{5} > \frac{2}{3}$

B. $\frac{3}{7} < \frac{2}{5}$

C. $\frac{5}{8} > \frac{6}{10}$

D. $\frac{4}{7} > \frac{6}{9}$

3) For what price is 20 percent off the same as $75 off?

A. $200

B. $300

C. $350

D. $375

4) If Manuel deposits 25% of $130 into a saving account, what is the amount of his deposit?

A. $5.20

B. $25.00

C. $32.50

D. $97.50

5) $\dfrac{1\frac{5}{4} + \frac{1}{3}}{2\frac{1}{2} - \frac{15}{8}}$ is approximately equal to.

A. 4.133

B. 4.6

C. 5.67

D. 6.33

6) What is $1.578 + 0.017 + 11.104$?

A. 12.699

B. 12.659

C. 11,896

D. 11,989

7) What is the value of 9.85×3.6?

A. 34.12

B. 34.65

C. 35.55

D. 35.46

8) If 80% of a number is 400, then what is 40% of that number?

A. 200

B. 320

C. 400

D. 500

9) What is the remainder when 754 is divided by 7?

A. 2

B. 3

C. 5

D. 6

10) Which of the following fractions is less than $\frac{3}{2}$?

A. 1.3

B. $\frac{5}{2}$

C. 3.01

D. 2.7

11) The average of five numbers is 37. If a sixth number 43 is added, then, what is the new average?

A. 38

B. 36

C. 29

D. 25

12) 15% of what number is equal to 75?

A. 8.64

B. 36

C. 300

D. 500

13) 45 people took the driving test and 18 of them passed. What percent of them failed the test?

A. 25%

B. 40%

C. 60%

D. 75%

14) Robert put $2,500 into a savings account that earns 3% in interest. How much will he have after 3 years?

A. $210

B. $225

C. $310

D. $335

15) What is the value of $\frac{8}{2} \div \frac{4}{7}$?

A. 4

B. 7

C. 16

D. 28

16) Which of the following fraction is equal to 0.009?

A. $\frac{1}{9}$

B. $\frac{9}{10}$

C. $\frac{9}{100}$

D. $\frac{9}{1,000}$

17) Jack earns $616 for his first 44 hours of work in a week and is then paid 1.5 times his regular hourly rate for any additional hours. This week, Jack needs $826 to pay his rent, bills and other expenses. How many hours must he work to make enough money in this week?

A. 40

B. 48

C. 53

D. 54

18) $1\frac{2}{3} + 2\frac{1}{6} - 2\frac{1}{3} - 1\frac{1}{6}$?

A. $\frac{1}{2}$

B. $\frac{1}{3}$

C. $\frac{2}{3}$

D. $\frac{1}{6}$

$$\frac{3}{8}, \frac{2}{5}, \frac{9}{20}, 37\%, 0.0375$$

19) Which of the following correctly orders the values above from greatest to least?

A. $\frac{9}{20}, \frac{3}{8}, \frac{2}{5}, 37\%, 0.0375$

B. $\frac{2}{5}, \frac{9}{20}, 37\%, \frac{3}{8}, 0.0375$

C. $\frac{9}{20}, \frac{2}{5}, 0.0375, \frac{3}{8}, 37\%$

D. $\frac{9}{20}, \frac{2}{5}, \frac{3}{8}, 37\%, 0.0375$

20) Which of the following is equivalent to $\frac{3}{5}$?

A. 0.06

B. 0.25

C. 0.60

D. 1.4

STOP: This is the End of Section 1 of test 4.

Next Generation

Accuplacer Mathematics

Practice Test 4

2021-2022

Section 2:

Quantitative Reasoning, Algebra, And Statistics

(No Calculator)

20 questions

Total time for this section: No time limit.

You may NOT use a calculator on this Section.

(On a real Accuplacer test, there is an onscreen calculator to use on some questions.)

56

1) If a box contains red and blue balls in ratio of $2:3$, how many red balls are there if 75 blue balls are in the box?

A. 15

B. 40

C. 50

D. 60

2) Which of the following points lies on the line $x + 2y = 4$?

A. $(-2, 3)$

B. $(1, 2)$

C. $(-1, 3)$

D. $(-3, 4)$

3) The length of a rectangle is $\frac{3}{2}$ times its width. If the width is $30\ cm$, what is the perimeter of this rectangle?

A. $100\ cm$

B. $150\ cm$

C. $180\ cm$

D. $240\ cm$

4) Solve for $x: \frac{3x}{5} = 27$?

A. 16.2

B. 31

C. 45

D. 135

5) If $3x + y = 25$ and $x - z = 14$, what is the value of x?

A. 0

B. 5

C. 10

D. It cannot be determined from the information given

6) Solve for y: $2(9y + 3) = -3(2y + 2)$

A. $\frac{1}{2}$

B. $\frac{1}{24}$

C. -1

D. $-\frac{1}{2}$

7) Approximately, what is the perimeter of the below figure?($\pi = 3$)

A. 18 cm

B. 22 cm

C. 36 cm

D. 40 cm

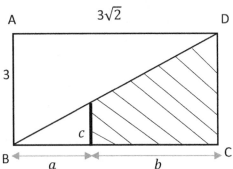

4 cm

8) Simplify $(3x - 5)^2$

A. $9x^2 + 30x + 25$

B. $9x^2 - 30x + 25$

C. $9x^2 + 25$

D. $9x^2 - 25$

9) What is the solution to equation $\frac{5}{2}x + \frac{1}{2}(2x + 1) - \frac{3}{2} = 3$?

A. $x = \frac{4}{3}$

B. $x = \frac{2}{7}$

C. $x = \frac{8}{7}$

D. $x = \frac{10}{7}$

10) In the following figure, ABCD is a rectangle. If $a = \sqrt{2}$, and $b = 2a$, find the area of the shaded region. (the shaded region is a trapezoid)

A. $2\sqrt{2}$

B. $4\sqrt{2}$

C. $5\sqrt{2}$

D. $6\sqrt{2}$

11) What is the solution of the following inequality? $|x - 9| \le 5$

A. $-14 \le x \le 14$

B. $-4 \le x \le 14$

C. $4 \le x \le 14$

D. $-14 \le x \le 4$

12) A number is chosen at random from 1 to 20. Find the probability of not selecting a composite number?

A. $\frac{1}{2}$

B. $\frac{7}{20}$

C. $\frac{9}{20}$

D. $\frac{11}{52}$

13) The mean of the following set is 10. What is the value of x? $\{9, 6, 12, 4x - 3, 10\}$

A. 8

B. 6

C. 5

D. 4

14) Solve $C = \frac{t - R}{s}$ for R.

A. $R = Cs - t$

B. $R = t - Cs$

C. $R = Cs + t$

D. $R = t + Cs$

15) The ratio of black cars to white cars in a parking lot is $3 : 8$. If there are 66 cars in the parking, how many more black cars should be added to make the ratio $1 : 1$?

A. 6

B. 18

C. 20

D. 30

16) What is the value of y in the following equation?

$$\frac{5}{8} - \frac{1}{4}y = \frac{1}{2}$$

A. 6

B. $\frac{1}{4}$

C. $\frac{1}{3}$

D. $\frac{1}{2}$

17) If the perimeter of the following figure be 33, what is the value of x

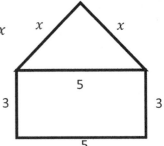

A. 4

B. 6

C. 8

D. 11

18) Perform the indicated operation and write the result in standard form:

$$(-5 + 10i)(-3 - 13i)$$

A. $145 + 95i$

B. $115 + 95i$

C. $115 + 20i$

D. $145 + 35i$

19) What is the equivalent temperature of $140°F$ in Celsius?

$$C = \frac{5}{9}(F - 32)$$

A. 32

B. 60

C. 68

D. 72

20) Simplify $7x^2y^3(2x^2y)^3 =$

A. $12x^4y^6$

B. $12x^8y^6$

C. $56x^4y^6$

D. $56x^8y^6$

STOP: This is the End of Section 2 of test 4.

Next Generation

Accuplacer Mathematics

Practice Test 4

2021-2022

Section 3:
Advanced Algebra and Functions
(Calculator)

20 questions

Total time for this section: No time limit.

You may use a calculator on this Section.

(On a real Accuplacer test, there is an onscreen calculator to use on some questions.)

61

1) If $\frac{3y-6}{7} = B$ and $B = 6$, what is the value of y?

A. 12

B. 16

C. 18

D. 21

2) Which of the following equations is equivalent to $3^{2x} = 5$?

A. $x = \frac{log_3 5}{2}$

B. $x = \frac{log_5 2}{3}$

C. $x = \frac{log_2 3}{5}$

D. $x = log_3 \left(\frac{5}{2}\right)$

3) Find side AC in the following triangle. Round your answer to the nearest tenth?

A. 6.6

B. 5.5

C. 4.5

D. 3.9

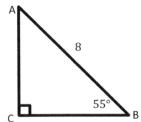

4) For $i = \sqrt{-1}$, which of the following is equivalent of $\frac{2+3i}{5-2i}$?

A. $\frac{3+2i}{5}$

B. $5 + 3i$

C. $\frac{4+19i}{29}$

D. $\frac{4+19i}{20}$

5) Find the equation of the horizontal asymptote of the function $f(x) = \frac{x+2}{x^2+1}$

A. $y = 0$

B. $y = -1$

C. $x = 1$

D. $y = 2x$

6) Find the solution (x, y) to the following system of equations?

$$-3x - y = 6$$
$$6x + 4y = 10$$

A. $(14, 5)$

B. $(6, 8)$

C. $(11, 17)$

D. $(-\frac{17}{3}, 11)$

7) Calculate $f(3)$ for the function $f(x) = 3x^2 - 4$.

A. 23

B. 30

C. 48

D. 50

8) What is the sum of all values of n that satisfies $2n^2 + 16n + 24 = 0$?

A. 8

B. 4

C. −4

D. −8

9) The graph of $y = f(x)$ is shown in the xy-plane below. Which the following equations could define $f(x)$?

A. $x^2 + 2x - 3$

B. $-x^2 - 2x + 3$

C. $(x - 2)(x + 3)$

D. $(x - 1)^2 + 3$

10) Find the value of x in the following diagram. (there are 2 supplementary angles in the diagram?

A. 60

B. 43

C. 45

D. 47

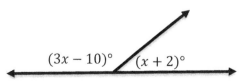

$(3x - 10)°$ $(x + 2)°$

11) The function $g(x)$ is defined by a polynomial. Some values of x and $g(x)$ are shown in the table below. Which of the following must be a factor of $g(x)$?

A. x

B. $x + 1$

C. $x - 1$

D. $x + 3$

x	$g(x)$
0	3
1	0
2	-3
3	-8
4	-12

12) What is the value of $\frac{6b}{c}$ when $\frac{c}{b} = 2$

A. 6

B. 4

C. 3

D. 1

13) Which of the following is equivalent to $\frac{x+(5x)^2+(3x)^3}{x}$?

A. $16x^2 + 25x + 1$

B. $27x^2 + 25x + 1$

C. $16x^2 + 25x$

D. $27x^3 + 16x^2 + 1$

14) If $\frac{c-b}{c} = \frac{24}{27}$, then which of the following must be true?

A. $\frac{b}{c} = \frac{1}{9}$

B. $\frac{b}{c} = \frac{17}{9}$

C. $\frac{b}{c} = \frac{24}{27}$

D. $\frac{b}{c} = \frac{21}{27}$

15) Which of the following lines is parallel to: $5y - 3x = 45$

A. $y = \frac{3}{5}x + 9$

B. $y = \frac{1}{3}x + 3$

C. $y = x - 2$

D. $y = 2x - 1$

16) What is the average of $4x + 2, -6x - 5$ and $8x + 2$?

A. $3x + 2$

B. $3x - 2$

C. $2x + 1$

D. $2x - \dfrac{1}{3}$

17) A rectangle was altered by increasing its length by 20 percent and decreasing its width by s percent. If these alterations decreased the area of the rectangle by 4 percent, what is the value of s?

A. 40

B. 31

C. 20

D. 10

18) Tickets for a talent show cost $3 for children and $4 for adults. If John spends at least $10 but no more than $15 on x children tickets and 2 adult ticket, what are two possible values of x?

A. $0, 1$

B. $1, 2$

C. $1, 4$

D. $1, 5$

19) If the interior angles of a quadrilateral are in the ratio $1 : 4 : 6 : 7$, what is the measure of the smallest angle?

A. $18°$

B. $20°$

C. $72°$

D. $120°$

20) What is the vertical asymptote of the graph $= \dfrac{4x-2}{3x+5}$?

A. $y = -\dfrac{1}{2}$

B. $y = \dfrac{3}{5}$

C. $x = \dfrac{3}{10}$

D. $x = -\dfrac{5}{3}$

STOP: This is the End of Test 4.

Next Generation

Accuplacer Mathematics

Practice Test 5

2021-2022

Section 1:
Arithmetic

(No Calculator)

20 questions

Total time for this section: No time limit.

You may NOT use a calculator on this Section.

(On a real Accuplacer test, there is an onscreen calculator to use on some questions.)

1) Evaluate
$$17[23 - (1 + 2)^2]$$

A. 238

B. 442

C. 540

D. 544

2) In two successive years, the population of a town is increased by 10% and 25%. What percent of the population is increased after two years?

A. 68%

B. 37.5%

C. 32%

D. 28%

3) Multiply and write the product in scientific notation
$$(1.7 \times 10^9) \times (2.9 \times 10^{-7})$$

A. 3.91×10

B. 0.391×10^2

C. 39.1×10^2

D. 3.91×10^2

4) What is 5 percent of 460?

A. 10

B. 18

C. 23

D. 40

5) The number 40.5 is 1,000 times greater than which of the following numbers?

A. 0.405

B. 0.0405

C. 0.0450

D. 0.00405

6) What is the value of $59,767,544.5 \times 0.00001$?

A. 597.675445

B. $59.767544.5$

C. $5.9767544.5$

D. $0.59767544.5$

7) What is the value of $\frac{6}{15} - \frac{4}{30} =$?

A. $\frac{1}{15}$

B. $\frac{2}{15}$

C. $\frac{4}{15}$

D. $\frac{8}{15}$

8) Which of the following is a correct statement?

A. $2\% < \frac{1}{20}$

B. $\frac{7}{8} < 0.8$

C. $3.5 < \frac{7}{3}$

D. $\frac{2}{6} > \frac{3}{8}$

9) What number is 35 more than 18% of 150?

A. 27

B. 52

C. 62

D. 72

10) 87 is equal to which of the following statements?

A. $\left(9 \times \frac{8}{2}\right) + \left(\frac{2}{8} \times 4\right) + 50$

B. $10 + \left(9 \times \frac{8}{2}\right) + \left(9 \times 4\right)$

C. $\left(4 \times 13\right) + \left(9 \times \frac{8}{2}\right)$

D. $2 + \left(3 \times 10\right) + \left(2 \times 30\right) - 20$

11) What is the remainder when 859 is divided by 9?

A. 0

B. 4

C. 6

D. 9

12) 15% of what number is equal to 90?

A. 8.64

B. 36

C. 300

D. 600

13) All of the following are ways to write 50 percent of A expect

A. $0.5A$

B. $\frac{50A}{100}$

C. $\frac{1}{2}A$

D. $0.05A$

14) Emma deposited $7,500 for two years into a money market account. At the end of two years she had a total of $8,700. What rate of interest did she receive?

A. 7%

B. 8%

C. 6%

D. 5%

15) What is the value of the "2" in 851.251?

A. 2 tenth

B. 2 hundredths

C. 2 tens

D. 2 thousandths

16) What is the value of $\frac{6}{4} + \frac{4}{8} + \frac{3}{2}$?

A. 4

B. $\frac{13}{8}$

C. $\frac{5}{8}$

D. $\frac{7}{2}$

17) A school wants to give each of its 22 top students a football ball. If the balls are in boxes of four, how many boxes of balls they need to purchase

A. 2

B. 4

C. 5

D. 6

18) Express in scientific notation: 0.00095

A. 9.5×10^{-3}

B. 9.5×10^{3}

C. 9.5×10^{-4}

D. 9.5×10^{4}

19) $12.124 \div 0.002$?

A. 6.0620

B. 60.620

C. 606.20

D. 6,062.0

20) Which of the following is equivalent to $\frac{4}{5}$?

A. 0.06

B. 0.25

C. 0.80

D. 1.4

STOP: This is the End of Section 1 of test 5.

Next Generation

Accuplacer Mathematics

Practice Test 5

2021-2022

Section 2:
Quantitative Reasoning, Algebra, And Statistics
(No Calculator)

20 questions

Total time for this section: No time limit.

You may NOT use a calculator on this Section.

(On a real Accuplacer test, there is an onscreen calculator to use on some questions.)

72

1) In the following figure, MN is 40 cm. How long is ON?

A. 25 cm

B. 20 cm

C. 15 cm

D. 10 cm

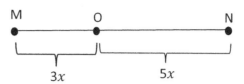

2) Which of the following could be the value of x if $\frac{5}{9} + x > 2$?

A. $\frac{1}{2}$

B. $\frac{3}{5}$

C. $\frac{4}{5}$

D. $\frac{5}{3}$

3) Evaluate $\frac{a^2 - b^2}{a - b}$ when $a = 6$ and $b = -3$.

A. 3

B. 9

C. $\frac{13}{3}$

D. 15

4) If the ratio of $5a$ to $2b$ is $\frac{1}{10}$, what is the ratio of a to b?

A. $\frac{1}{2}$

B. $\frac{1}{5}$

C. $\frac{1}{25}$

D. $\frac{1}{20}$

5) If 60% of x equal to 30% of 20, then what is the value of $(x + 5)^2$?

A. 25.25

B. 26

C. 26.01

D. 225

6) Find all of the polynomial factors of the binomial: $x^2 - 36$?

A. $(x - 3)(x + 3)$

B. $(x - 4)(x + 9)$

C. $(x^2 - 4x + 36)$

D. $(x - 6)(x + 6)$

7) If the following equations are true, what is the value of m?
$$a = \sqrt{2}$$
$$3a = \sqrt{3m}$$

A. $2\sqrt{3}$

B. 6

C. $3\sqrt{5}$

D. 9

8) If $4x + y = 25$ and $x - 2z = 24$, what is the value of x?

A. 0

B. 5

C. 10

D. It cannot be determined from the information given

9) Which of the following expressions is equivalent to $16 - \frac{2}{5}x \geq 8$

A. $x \geq 40$

B. $x \leq 40$

C. $x \geq 20$

D. $x \leq 20$

10) Solve for x: $2 + \frac{3x}{x-5} = \frac{3}{5-x}$?

A. $\frac{6}{5}$

B. $\frac{7}{5}$

C. $\frac{8}{5}$

D. $\frac{9}{5}$

11) If $y = 2ab + 3b^3$, what is the value of y, when $a = 3$ and $b = 5$?

A. 58

B. 90

C. 105

D. 405

12) Which of the following is equivalent to $-2 + \frac{3b-4c}{9b} - \frac{2b+2c}{6b}$?

A. $\frac{-18b-7c}{9b}$

B. $\frac{18b-7c}{9b}$

C. $\frac{-18b-14c}{18b}$

D. $\frac{-18b-7c}{18b}$

13) If $a \times b$ is divisible by 3, which of the following expression must also be divisible by 3?

A. $3a - b$

B. $a - 3b$

C. $\frac{a}{b}$

D. $4 \times a \times b$

14) How many tiles of $8\ cm^2$ is needed to cover a floor of dimension $6\ cm$ by $24\ cm$?

A. 6

B. 18

C. 55

D. 65

15) Solve for a.
$$-3a + 8(a + 8) = 49$$

A. $+3$

B. -3

C. -5

D. $+5$

16) If $\dfrac{25}{A} + 1 = 6$, then $25 + A = ?$

A. 5

B. $\dfrac{1}{4}$

C. 25

D. 30

17) What fraction of the following rectangle's area is shaded?

A. $\dfrac{3}{5}$

B. $\dfrac{2}{5}$

C. $\dfrac{2}{3}$

D. $\dfrac{4}{5}$

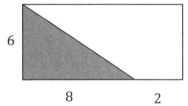

6

8   2

18) Michelle and Alec can finish a job together in 100 minutes. If Michelle can do the job by herself in 300 minutes, how many minutes does it take Alec to finish the job?

A. 190 *minutes*

B. 180 *minutes*

C. 160 *minutes*

D. 150 *minutes*

19) If $\sqrt{6n - 5} = n$, what is the values of n?

A. $(-5,1)$

B. $(5,1)$

C. $(5,6)$

D. $(-5,6)$

20) Simplify this rational expression: $\dfrac{7x}{x+4} \div \dfrac{x}{2x+8}$

A. 1

B. $\dfrac{7}{x+2}$

C. $\dfrac{14x}{x+4}$

D. 14

STOP: This is the End of Section 2 of test 5.

Next Generation

Accuplacer Mathematics

Practice Test 5

2021-2022

Section 3:
Advanced Algebra and Functions
(Calculator)

20 questions

Total time for this section: No time limit.

You may use a calculator on this Section.

(On a real Accuplacer test, there is an onscreen calculator to use on some questions.)

1) If x is a real number, and if $x^3 + 18 = 130$, then x lies between which two consecutive integers?

A. 1 and 2

B. 2 and 3

C. 3 and 4

D. 4 and 5

2) If $\frac{3y}{25} = \frac{y-1}{5}$, $y =?$

A. $\frac{1}{5}$

B. $\frac{5}{2}$

C. 3

D. 5

3) If $(x - 2)^3 = 27$ which of the following could be the value of $(x - 6)(x - 4)$?

A. 1

B. 2

C. 6

D. -1

4) If cotangent of an angel α is 2, then the tangent of angle α is?

A. 1

B. 2

C. -2

D. $\frac{1}{2}$

5) What is the value of x in this equation?
$$4\sqrt{2x + 9} = 28$$

A. 7

B. 20

C. 28

D. 40

6) Find the value of y in the following system of equations?

$$3x - 4y = -20$$
$$-x + 2y = 10$$

A. -2

B. 2

C. -5

D. 5

7) What is the ratio of the minimum value to the maximum value of the following function?
$$f(x) = -2x + 1; -3 \le x \le 2$$

A. $-\dfrac{3}{7}$

B. $-\dfrac{5}{7}$

C. $+\dfrac{3}{7}$

D. $+\dfrac{5}{7}$

8) What are the zeroes of the function $f(x) = x^3 + 8x^2 + 12x$?

A. 2

B. 6

C. $0, 2, 6$

D. $0, -2, -6$

9) Point A lies on the line with equation $y - 2 = 3(x + 2)$. If the x-coordinate of A is 6, what is the y-coordinate of A?

A. 22

B. 24

C. 26

D. 28

10) In the triangle below, if the measure of angle A is 49 degrees, then what is the value of y? (figure is NOT drawn to scale)

A. 27

B. 43

C. 56

D. 64

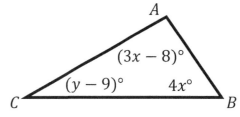

11) The function $g(x)$ is defined by a polynomial. Some values of x and $g(x)$ are shown in the table below. Which of the following must be a factor of $g(x)$?

A. $x - 2$

B. $x - 1$

C. $x + 2$

D. $x + 1$

x	$g(x)$
-1	4
-2	0
0	5
1	4
2	6

12) Solve this equation for x: $e^{3x} = 18$

A. 18

B. $ln(18)$

C. $\dfrac{ln(18)}{3}$

D. $\dfrac{e^{3x}}{4}$

13) $\dfrac{\frac{1}{4}+1\frac{1}{3}-1\frac{1}{2}}{2\frac{1}{3}+1\frac{1}{3}-3\frac{1}{3}}$ is approximately equal to

A. 0.01

B. 0.25

C. 1.25

D. 9.25

14) The inequality $|x + 5| \geq 2$ is equivalent to?

A. $x \leq -7$

B. $x \geq -7$

C. $x \leq -7 \; or \; x \geq -3$

D. $-3 \geq x \geq -7$

15) What is the center and radius of a circle with the following equation?
$$(x - 3)^2 + (y + 5)^2 = 5$$

A. $C(3, -5), r = \sqrt{5}$

B. $C(-3, 5), r = \sqrt{5}$

C. $C(3, -5), r = 5$

D. $C(-3, 5), r = 5$

16) What is the average of $2y + 4, 4y - 3, -y + 3$ and $3y - 1$?

A. $2y + 1$

B. $2y - \frac{3}{4}$

C. $2y + \frac{3}{4}$

D. $3y - \frac{1}{4}$

17) If $f(x) = 7x - 5$ and $g(x) = 2x^2 - 4x$, then find $(\frac{f}{g})(x)$.

A. $\frac{7x-5}{2x^2-4x}$

B. $\frac{x-1}{x^2-1}$

C. $\frac{2x-1}{x^2-2}$

D. $\frac{5x+5}{x^2+2x}$

18) If $f(x) = \frac{4x^2-6x+12}{9-x}$, which of the following is NOT defined?

A. $f(9)$

B. $f(0)$

C. $f(-4)$

D. $f(-9)$

19) Let r and p be constants. If $x^2 + 6x + r$ factors into $(x + 2)(x + p)$, the values of r and p respectively are?

A. 8 , 4

B. 4 , 8

C. 6 , 3

D. 3 , 6

20) Which of the following expressions is equal to $\sqrt{\frac{x^2}{2} + \frac{x^2}{16}}$?

A. x

B. $\frac{3x}{4}$

C. $x\sqrt{x}$

D. $\frac{x\sqrt{x}}{4}$

STOP: This is the End of Test 5.

Accuplacer Mathematics Practice Test Answers and Explanations

Now, it's time to review your results to see where you went wrong and what areas you need to improve!

Accuplacer Math Test 1

Arithmetic				Quantitative Reasoning, Algebra, And Statistics				Advanced Algebra and Functions			
1	D	16	C	1	C	16	B	1	C	16	B
2	A	17	C	2	A	17	B	2	A	17	A
3	D	18	B	3	C	18	B	3	C	18	C
4	B	19	C	4	C	19	B	4	C	19	C
5	C	20	C	5	D	20	A	5	C	20	B
6	C			6	A			6	A		
7	C			7	D			7	B		
8	A			8	D			8	D		
9	D			9	C			9	B		
10	B			10	A			10	B		
11	C			11	C			11	C		
12	D			12	B			12	D		
13	C			13	C			13	C		
14	B			14	B			14	C		
15	C			15	D			15	A		

Accuplacer Math Test 2

	Arithmetic				Quantitative Reasoning, Algebra, And Statistics					Advanced Algebra and Functions			
1	B	16	D	1	A	16	D	1	D	16	D
2	C	17	D	2	A	17	C	2	C	17	B
3	D	18	C	3	B	18	D	3	B	18	A
4	C	19	D	4	C	19	B	4	C	19	A
5	D	20	C	5	B	20	D	5	C	20	D
6	A			6	D			6	D		
7	D			7	B			7	A		
8	A			8	B			8	D		
9	C			9	D			9	D		
10	A			10	B			10	D		
11	A			11	A			11	C		
12	D			12	B			12	C		
13	D			13	D			13	B		
14	B			14	B			14	B		
15	A			15	D			15	A		

Accuplacer Math Test 3

	Arithmetic				Quantitative Reasoning, Algebra, And Statistics					Advanced Algebra and Functions			
1	D	16	B	1	C	16	B	1	C	16	B
2	A	17	C	2	D	17	B	2	A	17	A
3	D	18	B	3	C	18	B	3	D	18	A
4	B	19	C	4	C	19	D	4	C	19	C
5	D	20	D	5	C	20	A	5	C	20	B
6	C			6	A			6	A		
7	D			7	D			7	C		
8	A			8	C			8	D		
9	D			9	C			9	B		
10	B			10	D			10	D		
11	C			11	C			11	C		
12	D			12	B			12	D		
13	C			13	C			13	C		
14	B			14	B			14	C		
15	C			15	C			15	C		

Accuplacer Math Test 4

	Arithmetic				Quantitative Reasoning, Algebra, And Statistics				Advanced Algebra and Functions		
1	B	16	D	1	C	16	D	1	B	16	D
2	C	17	D	2	A	17	D	2	A	17	C
3	D	18	B	3	B	18	D	3	A	18	B
4	C	19	D	4	C	19	B	4	C	19	B
5	A	20	C	5	D	20	D	5	A	20	D
6	A			6	D			6	D		
7	D			7	B			7	A		
8	A			8	B			8	D		
9	C			9	C			9	A		
10	A			10	B			10	D		
11	A			11	C			11	C		
12	D			12	C			12	C		
13	C			13	D			13	B		
14	B			14	B			14	A		
15	B			15	D			15	A		

Accuplacer Math Test 5

	Arithmetic				Quantitative Reasoning, Algebra, And Statistics				Advanced Algebra and Functions		
1	A	16	D	1	A	16	D	1	D	16	C
2	B	17	D	2	D	17	B	2	B	17	A
3	D	18	C	3	A	18	D	3	D	18	A
4	C	19	D	4	C	19	B	4	D	19	A
5	B	20	C	5	D	20	D	5	B	20	B
6	A			6	A			6	D		
7	C			7	B			7	A		
8	A			8	D			8	D		
9	C			9	D			9	C		
10	A			10	B			10	D		
11	B			11	D			11	C		
12	D			12	A			12	C		
13	D			13	D			13	B		
14	B			14	B			14	C		
15	A			15	B			15	A		

ACCUPLACER Mathematics Practice Test 1

Arithmetic

1) Choice D is correct

A. $24 \times \frac{1}{4} = \frac{24}{4} = 6 = 6$

B. $2 \times \frac{6}{2} = \frac{12}{2} = 6 = 6$

C. $5 \times \frac{6}{5} = \frac{30}{5} = 6 = 6$

D. $6 \times \frac{1}{6} = \frac{6}{6} = 1 \neq 6$

2) Choice A is correct

First multiply the tenths place of 7.8 by 3.56. The result is 2.848. Next, multiply 7 by 3.56 which results in 24.92. The sum of these two numbers is: $2.848 + 24.92 = 27.768$

3) Choice D is correct

Dividing 85 by 20%, which is equivalent to 0.2, gives 425. Therefore, 20% of 425 is 85.

4) Choice B is correct

$\frac{12}{8} = 1.5$, the only choice that is greater than 1.5 is $\frac{5}{2}$. $\frac{5}{2} = 2.5$, $2.5 > 1.5$

5) Choice C is correct

$\$10 \times 10 = \$100$, Petrol use:$10 \times 2 = 20$ liters

Petrol cost: $20 \times \$1 = \$20$. Money earned:$\$100 - \$20 = \$80$

6) Choice C is correct

The closest to 5.03 is 5 in the options provided.

7) Choice C is correct

Let x be the original price. If the price of the sofa is decreased by 15% to $476, then:
$85\%\ of\ x = 476 \Rightarrow 0.85x = 476 \Rightarrow x = 476 \div 0.85 = 560$

8) Choice A is correct

The percent of girls playing tennis is: $40\% \times 25\% = 0.40 \times 0.25 = 0.10 = 10\%$

9) Choice D is correct

Write the equation and solve for B: $0.60\ A = 0.20\ B$, divide both sides by 0.20, then:
$\frac{0.60}{0.20}A = B$, therefore: $B = 3A$, and B is 3 times of A or it's 300% of A.

10) Choice B is correct

Use this formula: Percent of Change $\dfrac{New\ Value - Old\ Value}{Old\ Value} \times 100\%$

$\dfrac{16,000-20,000}{20,000} \times 100\% = -20\%$ and $\dfrac{12,800-16,000}{16,000} \times 100\% = -20\%$

11) Choice C is correct

Use simple interest formula: $I = prt(I = interest,\ p = principal, r = rate, t = time)$

$I = (8,000)(0.045)(5) = 1,800$

12) Choice D is correct

A. $x = \dfrac{1}{3} \to \dfrac{6}{8} + \dfrac{1}{3} = \dfrac{18+8}{24} = \dfrac{26}{24} \approx 1.083 < 2$

B. $x = \dfrac{3}{5} \to \dfrac{6}{8} + \dfrac{3}{5} = \dfrac{30+24}{40} = \dfrac{54}{40} \approx 1.35 < 2$

C. $x = \dfrac{6}{5} \to \dfrac{6}{8} + \dfrac{6}{5} = \dfrac{30+48}{40} = \dfrac{78}{40} \approx 1.95 < 2$

D. $x = \dfrac{4}{3} \to \dfrac{6}{8} + \dfrac{4}{3} = \dfrac{18+32}{24} = \dfrac{50}{24} \approx 2.08 > 2$

Only choice D works in the inequality.

13) Choice C is correct

$\dfrac{25}{20} = 1.25 = 125\%$

14) Choice B is correct

To add decimal numbers, line them up and add from right.

$2.85 + 0.045 + 0.1265 = 3.0215$

15) Choice C is correct

Use distance formula: $Distance = Rate \times time \Rightarrow 420 = 50 \times T$, divide both sides by 50. Then: $420 \div 50 = T \Rightarrow T = 8.4\ hours$.

Change hours to minutes for the decimal part. $0.4\ hours = 0.4 \times 60 = 24\ minutes$.

16) Choice C is correct

Let's compare each fraction: $\dfrac{2}{7} < \dfrac{3}{8} < \dfrac{5}{11} < \dfrac{3}{4}$. Only choice C provides the right order.

17) Choice C is correct.

$\dfrac{4}{5} - \dfrac{3}{5} = \dfrac{1}{5} = 0.2$

18)Choice B is correct

$x = \frac{530.40}{624} = 0.85 = 85\%$. 530.40 is 85% of 624. Therefore, the discount is:

$100\% - 85\% = 15\%$

19)Choice C is correct

The weight of 12.2 meters of this rope is: $12.2 \times 600\ g = 7,320\ g$

$1\ kg = 1,000\ g$, therefore, $7,320\ g \div 1,000 = 7.32\ kg$

20)Choice C is correct.

$\frac{91501}{305} \approx 300.0032 \approx 300$

Accuplacer Mathematics Practice Test 1

Quantitative Reasoning, Algebra, And Statistics

1) Choice C is correct

Let x be the number. Write the equation and solve for x. $(24 - x) \div x = 3$

Multiply both sides by x. $(24 - x) = 3x$, then add x both sides. $24 = 4x$, now divide both sides by 4. $x = 6$

2) Choice A is correct

The sum of supplement angles is 180. Let x be that angle. Therefore, $x + 9x = 180$

$10x = 180$, divide both sides by 10: $x = 18$

3) Choice C is correct

The average speed of john is: $150 \div 6 = 25 \, km$. The average speed of Alice is: $180 \div 4 = 45 \, km$. Write the ratio and simplify. $25 : 45 = 5 : 9$

4) Choice C is correct

$\dfrac{30}{A} + 1 = 7 \rightarrow \dfrac{30}{A} = 7 - 1 = 6 \rightarrow 30 = 6A \rightarrow A = \dfrac{30}{6} = 5 \rightarrow 30 + A = 30 + 5 = 35$

5) Choice D is correct

Use Pythagorean Theorem: $a^2 + b^2 = c^2$

$9^2 + 12^2 = c^2 \Rightarrow 81 + 144 = c^2 \Rightarrow 225 = c^2 \Rightarrow c = 15$

6) Choice A is correct

Area of the circle is less than 16π. Use the formula of areas of circles.

$Area = \pi r^2 \Rightarrow 64\,\pi > \pi r^2 \Rightarrow 64 > r^2 \Rightarrow r < 8$

Radius of the circle is less than 8. Let's put 8 for the radius. Now, use the circumference formula: $Circumference = 2\pi r = 2\pi\,(8) = 16\,\pi$

Since the radius of the circle is less than 8. Then, the circumference of the circle must be less than 16π. Only choice A is less than 16π.

7) Choice D is correct

If the length of the box is 27, then the width of the box is one third of it, 9, and the height of the box is 3 (one third of the width). The volume of the box is:

$V = lwh = (27)(9)(3) = 729$

8) Choice D is correct

To find the number of possible outfit combinations, multiply number of options for each factor: $6 \times 3 \times 5 = 90$

9) Choice C is correct

Since E is the midpoint of AB, then the area of all triangles DAE, DEF, CFE and CBE are equal. Let x be the area of one of the triangle, then: $4x = 100 \rightarrow x = 25$

The area of $DEC = 2x = 2(25) = 50$

10) Choice A is correct

The equation of a line in slope intercept form is: $y = mx + b$, Solve for y.

$2x - 4y = 24 \Rightarrow -4y = 24 - 2x \Rightarrow y = (24 - 2x) \div (-4) \Rightarrow y = \frac{1}{2}x - 6$

The slope is $\frac{1}{2}$. The slope of the line perpendicular to this line is:

$$m_1 \times m_2 = -1 \Rightarrow \frac{1}{2} \times m_2 = -1 \Rightarrow m_2 = -2$$

11) Choice C is correct

Let x be the number. Write the equation and solve for x.

$\frac{2}{3} \times 18 = \frac{2}{5} . x \Rightarrow \frac{2 \times 18}{3} = \frac{2x}{5}$, use cross multiplication to solve for x.

$5 \times 36 = 2x \times 3 \Rightarrow 180 = 6x \Rightarrow x = 30$

12) Choice B is correct

Use the information provided in the question to draw the shape.

Use Pythagorean Theorem: $a^2 + b^2 = c^2$

$40^2 + 30^2 = c^2 \Rightarrow 1,600 + 900 = c^2 \Rightarrow 2,500 = c^2 \Rightarrow c = 50$

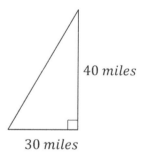

40 *miles*

30 *miles*

13) Choice C is correct

The ratio of boy to girls is 4: 7. Therefore, there are 4 boys out of 11 students. To find the answer, first divide the total number of students by 11, then multiply the result by 4. $44 \div 11 = 4 \Rightarrow 4 \times 4 = 16$. There are 16 boys and $28 = (44 - 16)$ girls. So, 12 more boys should be enrolled to make the ratio 1: 1

14) Choice B is correct

If the score of Mia was 60, therefore the score of Ava is 30. Since the score of Emma was half as that of Ava, therefore, the score of Emma is 15.

15) Choice D is correct

If 17 balls are removed from the bag at random, there will be one ball in the bag. The probability of choosing a brown ball is 1 out of 18. Therefore, the probability of not choosing a brown ball is 17 out of 18 and the probability of having not a brown ball after removing 17 balls is the same.

16) Choice B is correct

Let x be the smallest number. Then, these are the numbers:

$x, x + 1, x + 2, x + 3, x + 4$

$$average = \frac{sum\ of\ terms}{number\ of\ terms} \Rightarrow 38 = \frac{x + (x + 1) + (x + 2) + (x + 3) + (x + 4)}{5} \Rightarrow$$

$$38 = \frac{5x + 10}{5} \Rightarrow 190 = 5x + 10 \Rightarrow 180 = 5x \Rightarrow x = 36$$

17) Choice B is correct

$average = \frac{sum\ of\ terms}{number\ of\ terms}$. The sum of the weight of all girls is: $18 \times 60 = 1,080\ kg$

The sum of the weight of all boys is: $32 \times 62 = 1,984\ kg$, the sum of the weight of all students is: $1,080 + 1,984 = 3,064\ kg.\ average = \frac{3,064}{50} = 61.28$

18) Choice B is correct

Write the numbers in order:$4, 5, 8, 9, 13, 15, 18$. Since we have 7 numbers (7 is odd), then the median is the number in the middle, which is 9.

19) Choice B is correct

The Area that one liter of paint is required: $80cm \times 95cm = 7,600cm^2$

Remember: $1\ m^2 = 10,000\ cm^2(100 \times 100 = 10,000), then, 7,600cm^2 = 0.76\ m^2$

Number of liters of paint we need: $\frac{57}{0.76} = 75$ liters

20) Choice A is correct

Let x be the number of years. Therefore, $2,000 per year equals $2000x$. Starting from $24,000 annual salary means you should add that amount to $2000x$.

Income more than that is:$I > 2000x + 24000$

Accuplacer Mathematics Practice Test 1

Advanced Algebra and Functions

1) Choice C is correct

Method 1: Plugin the values of x and y provided in the choices into both equations. Let's start with $2x + 2y = 2$:

A. $(1, 3)$ $\quad$ $2x + 2y = 2 \rightarrow 2 + 6 \neq 2$

B. $(2, 4)$ $\quad$ $2x + y = 2 \rightarrow 4 + 8 \neq 2$

C. $(2, -1)$ $\quad$ $2x + 2y = 2 \rightarrow 4 + (-2) = 2$

D. $(4, -6)$ $\quad$ $2x + 2y = 2 \rightarrow 12 + (-12) \neq 2$

Only choice C is correct.

2) Choice A is correct

If $f(x) = 3x + 4(x + 1) + 2$, then find $f(4x)$ by substituting $4x$ for every x in the function. This gives: $f(4x) = 3(4x) + 4(4x + 1) + 2$

It simplifies to: $f(4x) = 3(4x) + 4(4x + 1) + 2 = 12x + 16x + 4 + 2 = 28x + 6$.

3) Choice C is correct

First, find the equation of the line. All lines through the origin are of the form $y = mx$, so the equation is $y = \frac{1}{3}x$. Of the given choices, only choice C $(9,3)$, satisfies this equation: $y = \frac{1}{3}x \rightarrow 3 = \frac{1}{3}(9) = 3$.

4) Choice C is correct

$(3n^2 + 2n + 6) - (2n^2 - 4)$. Add like terms together: $3n^2 - 2n^2 = n^2$, $2n$ doesn't have like terms. $6 - (-4) = 10$, Combine these terms into one expression to find the answer: $n^2 + 2n + 10$.

5) Choice C is correct

Simplify and solve for x in the equation. $4(x + 1) = 6(x - 4) + 20$, $4x + 4 = 6x - 24 + 20$, $4x + 4 = 6x - 4$. Subtract $4x$ from both sides: $4 = 2x - 4$, Add 4 to both sides:

$8 = 2x$, $4 = x$.

6) Choice A is correct

To rewrite $\dfrac{1}{\frac{1}{x-5}+\frac{1}{x+4}}$, first simplify $\dfrac{1}{x-5}+\dfrac{1}{x+4}$.

$$\frac{1}{x-5}+\frac{1}{x+4}=\frac{1(x+4)}{(x-5)(x+4)}+\frac{1(x-5)}{(x+4)(x-5)}=\frac{(x+4)+(x-5)}{(x+4)(x-5)}$$

Then: $\dfrac{1}{\frac{1}{x-5}+\frac{1}{x+4}}=\dfrac{1}{\frac{(x+4)+(x-5)}{(x+4)(x-5)}}=\dfrac{(x-5)(x+4)}{(x-5)+(x+4)}$. (Remember, $\frac{1}{\frac{1}{x}}=x$)

This result is equivalent to the expression in choice A.

7) Choice B is correct

Since $(0,0)$ is a solution to the system of inequalities, substituting 0 for x and 0 for y in the given system must result in two true inequalities. After this substitution, $y < c - x$ becomes $0 < a$, and $y > x + b$ becomes $0 > b$. Hence, a is positive and b is negative. Therefore, $c > b$

8) Choice D is correct

$$3x + 10 = 46 \rightarrow 3x = 46 - 10 = 36 \rightarrow x = \frac{36}{3} = 12$$

9) Choice B is correct

The input value is 5. Then: $x = 5$

$$f(x) = x^2 - 3x \rightarrow f(5) = 5^2 - 3(5) = 25 - 15 = 10$$

10) Choice B is correct

To solve this problem, first recall the equation of a line: $y = mx + b$ Where $m = slope$. $y = y - $ intercept. Remember that slope is the rate of change that occurs in a function and that the $y -$ intercept is the y value corresponding to $x = 0$. Since the height of John's plant is 5 inches tall when he gets it. Time (or x) is zero. The plant grows 3 inches per year. Therefore, the rate of change of the plant's height is 3. The $y -$intercept represents the starting height of the plant which is 5 inches.

11) Choice C is correct

Multiplying each side of $\dfrac{4}{x}=\dfrac{12}{x-8}$ by $x(x-8)$ gives $4(x-8)=12(x)$, distributing the 4 over the values within the parentheses yields $x - 8 = 3x$ or $x = -4$. Therefore, the value of $\dfrac{x}{2}=\dfrac{-4}{2}=-2$.

12) Choice D is correct

The equation of a circle can be written as $(x - h)^2 + (y - k)^2 = r^2$ where (h, k) are the coordinates of the center of the circle and r is the radius of the circle. Since the coordinates of the center of the circle are $(-1, 2)$, the equation is

$(x + 1)^2 + (y - 2)^2 = r^2$, where r is the radius. The radius of the circle is the distance from the center $(-1, 2)$, to the given endpoint of a radius, $(2, 6)$. By the distance formula, $r^2 = (2 - (-1))^2 + (6 - 2)^2 = (3)^2 + (4)^2 = 9 + 16 = 25$, Therefore, an equation of the given circle is $(x + 1)^2 + (y - 2)^2 = 25$

13) Choice C is correct

To solve for $\cos A$ first identify what is known. The question states that ΔABC is a right triangle whose $\angle B = 90°$ and $\sin C = \frac{8}{17}$. It is important to recall that any triangle has a sum of interior angles that equals 180 degrees. Therefore, to calculate $\cos A$ use the complimentary angles identify of trigonometric function. $\cos A = \cos(90 - C)$, Then: $\cos A = \sin C$ For complementary angles, sin of one angle is equal to cos of the other angle. $\cos A = \frac{8}{17}$

14) Choice C is correct

Let x be all expenses, then $\frac{22}{100}x = \$660 \rightarrow x = \frac{100 \times \$660}{22} = \$3,000$

Mr. Green's spent for his rent: $\frac{27}{100} \times \$3,000 = \$810$

15) Choice A is correct

The amount of money for x bookshelf is: $200x$, Then, the total cost of all bookshelves is equal to: $200x + 600$, The total cost, in dollar, per bookshelf is:

$$\frac{Total\ cost}{number\ of\ items} = \frac{200x + 600}{x}$$

16) Choice B is correct

It is given that $g(5) = 4$. Therefore, to find the value of $f(g(5))$, then $f(g(5)) = f(4) = 6$

17) Choice A is correct

Area of the triangle is: $\frac{1}{2}AD \times BC$ and AD is perpendicular to BC.

Triangle ADC is a $30° - 60° - 90°$ right triangle.

The relationship among all sides of right triangle $30° - 60° - 90°$ is provided in the following triangle: In this triangle, the opposite side of $30°$ angle is half of the hypotenuse. And the opposite side of $60°$ is opposite of $30° \times \sqrt{3}$

$CD = 6$, then $AD = 6 \times \sqrt{3}$

Area of the triangle ABC is: $\frac{1}{2} AD \times BC = \frac{1}{2}(6\sqrt{3}) \times 12 = 36\sqrt{3}$

18) Choice C is correct

$6 \blacksquare 28 = \sqrt{6^2 + 28} = \sqrt{36 + 28} = \sqrt{64} = 8$

19) Choice C is correct

The equation of a circle with center (h, k) and radius r is$(x - h)^2 + (y - k)^2 = r^2$. To put the equation $x^2 + y^2 + 8x - 2y = 1$ in this form, complete the square as follows:

$x^2 + y^2 + 8x - 2y = 1, \quad (x^2 + 8x) + (y^2 - 2y) = 1,$

$(x^2 + 8x + 16) - 16 + (y^2 - 2y + 1) - 1 = 1, (x + 4)^2 + (y - 1)^2 = 18$

$(x + 4)^2 + (y - 1)^2 = (\sqrt{18})^2$

Therefore, the radius of the circle is $\sqrt{18}$. Simplify: $\sqrt{18}$. Then: $\sqrt{18} = \sqrt{9 \times 2} = 3\sqrt{2}$

20) Choice B is correct

Angle x is the sum of the other two angles provided. Then: $x = 20 + 125 = 145$

ACCUPLACER Mathematical Reasoning Practice Test 2

Arithmetic

1) Choice B is correct

$5 \text{ percent of } 480 = \dfrac{5}{100} \times 480 = \dfrac{1}{20} \times 480 = \dfrac{480}{20} = 24$

2) Choice C is correct

The population is increased by 15% and 20%. 15% increase changes the population to 115% of original population. For the second increase, multiply the result by 120%. $(1.15) \times (1.20) = 1.38 = 138\%$. 38 percent of the population is increased after two years.

3) Choice D is correct

$75 off is the same as 15 percent off. Thus, 15 percent of a number is 75.

Then: $15\% \ of \ x = 75 \rightarrow 0.15x = 75 \rightarrow x = \dfrac{75}{0.15} = 500$

4) Choice C is correct

Three times of 24,000 is 72,000. One sixth of them cancelled their tickets.

One sixth of 72,000 equals 12,000 $(\dfrac{1}{6} \times 72{,}000 = 12{,}000)$.

$60{,}000(72{,}000 - 12{,}000 = 60{,}000)$ fans are attending this week.

5) Choice D is correct

Change the numbers to decimal and then compare. $\dfrac{2}{3} = 0.666 \ldots$

$0.68, 67\% = 0.67, \dfrac{4}{5} = 0.80.$ Then: $\dfrac{2}{3} < 67\% < 0.68 < \dfrac{4}{5}$

Only choice D is correct.

6) Choice A is correct

To find the sum of two whole numbers, line the numbers up and add digits from right.

$$
\begin{array}{r}
12{,}181 \\
+ \ 8{,}591 \\
\hline
20{,}772
\end{array}
$$

7) Choice D is correct

15% of $160 is $0.15 \times 160 = 24$

8) Choice A is correct

First, find the number. Let x be the number. 150% of a number is 75, then:

$1.5 \times x = 75 \Rightarrow x = 75 \div 1.5 = 50$

90% of 50 is: $0.9 \times 50 = 45$

9) Choice C is correct

The result when 1,454 is divided by 7 is 207 with a remainder of 5. Multiplying $7 \times 207 = 1,449$ and $1,454 - 1,449 = 5$, which is the remainder.

10) Choice A is correct.

$\frac{3}{2} = 1.5$. The only choice less than 1.5 is 1.4. $\frac{3}{2} = 1.5 > 1.4$

11) Choice A is correct

2,500 out of 55,000 equals to $\frac{2500}{55000} = \frac{25}{550} = \frac{1}{22}$

12) Choice D is correct

Dividing 72 by 16%, which is equivalent to 0.16, gives 450.

13) Choice D is correct

The failing rate is 11 out of $55 = \frac{11}{55}$. Change the fraction to percent: $\frac{11}{55} \times 100\% = 20\%$

20 percent of students failed. Therefore, 80 percent of students passed the exam.

14) Choice B is correct

Solve for x. Then: $\frac{6}{5} \div \frac{1}{8} = x \rightarrow \frac{6}{5} \times \frac{8}{1} = \frac{48}{5} = 9.6$, Number 9.6 is between 8 and 10.

15) Choice A is correct.

The second digit to the right of the decimal point is in the hundredths place and the third number to the right of the decimal point is in the thousandths place. Since the number in the thousandths place of 0.5749, which is 4, is less than 5, the number 0.5749should be rounded down to 0.57

16) Choice D is correct

$\frac{3}{4} \times 28 = \frac{84}{4} = 21$

17) Choice D is correct

Ethan needs an 75% average to pass for five exams. Therefore, the sum of 5 exams must be at lease $5 \times 75 = 375$, The sum of 4 exams is: $68 + 72 + 85 + 90 = 315$.

The minimum score Jason can earn on his fifth and final test to pass is:

$375 - 315 = 60$

18) Choice C is correct

The second digit to the right of the decimal point is in the hundredths place and the third number to the right of the decimal point is in the thousandths place. Since the number in the thousandths place of 120.756, which is 6, is greater than 5, the number 120.756 should be rounded up to 120.76.

19) Choice D is correct

To best compare the numbers, they should be put in the same format. The percent 0.625% can be converted to a decimal by dividing 0.625 by 100, which gives 0.00625. $\frac{5}{8}$ can be converted to a decimal by dividing 5 by 8, which gives 0.625. Now, all three numbers are in decimal format. $0.625 > 0.0625 > 0.00625$ or $\frac{5}{8} > 0.0625 > 0.625\%$, which is choice D.

20) Choice C is correct

The fraction $\frac{2}{5}$ can be written as $\frac{2 \times 20}{5 \times 20} = \frac{40}{100}$, which can be interpreted as forty hundredths, or 0.40.

Accuplacer Mathematics Practice Test 2

Quantitative Reasoning, Algebra, And Statistics

1) Choice A is correct

In the stadium the ratio of home fans to visiting fans in a crowd is $5:7$. Therefore, the total number of fans must be divisible by 12: $5 + 7 = 12$. Let's review the choices:

A. 12,324 $12,324 \div 12 = 1,027$

B. 42,326 $42,326 \div 12 = 3,527.166$

C. 44,566 $44,566 \div 12 = 3,713.833$

D. 66,812 $66,812 \div 12 = 5,567.666$

Only choice A when divided by 12 results a whole number.

2) Choice A is correct

The equation of the line is: $2x - y = -6$. Plug in the values of x and y from choices provided. Then:

A. $(-1, 4)$ $2x - y = -6 \rightarrow 2(-1) - 4 = -6 \rightarrow -2 - 4 = -6$ This is true!

B. $(2, 2)$ $2x - y = -6 \rightarrow 2(2) - 2 = -6 \rightarrow 4 - 2 = -6$ This is NOT true!

C. $(1, 3)$ $2x - y = -6 \rightarrow 2(1) - 3 = -6 \rightarrow 2 - 3 = -6$ This is NOT true!

D. $(3, 1)$ $2x - y = -6 \rightarrow 2(3) - 1 = -6 \rightarrow 6 - 1 = -6$ This is NOT true!

3) Choice B is correct

A linear equation is a relationship between two variables, x and y, and can be written in the form of $y = mx + b$. A non-proportional linear relationship takes on the form $y = mx + b$, where $b \neq 0$ and its graph is a line that does not cross through the origin. Only in graph B, the line does not pass through the origin

4) Choice C is correct

$$average\ (mean) = \frac{sum\ of\ terms}{number\ of\ terms} \Rightarrow 88 = \frac{sum\ of\ terms}{50} \Rightarrow sum = 88 \times 50 = 4,400$$

The difference of 94 and 69 is 25. Therefore, 25 should be subtracted from the sum.

$$4,400 - 25 = 4,375,\ mean = \frac{sum\ of\ terms}{number\ of\ terms} \Rightarrow mean = \frac{4,375}{50} = 87.5$$

5) Choice B is correct

To get a sum of 6 for two dice, we can get 5 different options:

$(5,1),(4,2),(3,3),(2,4),(1,5)$, To get a sum of 9 for two dice, we can get 4 different options:$(6,3),(5,4),(4,5),(3,6)$. Therefore, there are 9 options to get the sum of 6 or 9. Since, we have $6 \times 6 = 36$ total options, the probability of getting a sum of 6 and 9 is 9 out of 36 or $\frac{1}{4}$.

6) Choice D is correct

Use formula of rectangle prism volume.

$V = (length)(width)(height) \Rightarrow 2,000 = (25)(10)(height) \Rightarrow height = 2,000 \div 250 = 8$

7) Choice B is correct

The diagonal of the square is 8. Let x be the side.

Use Pythagorean Theorem: $a^2 + b^2 = c^2$

$x^2 + x^2 = 8^2 \Rightarrow 2x^2 = 8^2 \Rightarrow 2x^2 = 64 \Rightarrow x^2 = 32 \Rightarrow x = \sqrt{32}$

The area of the square is:$\sqrt{32} \times \sqrt{32} = 32$

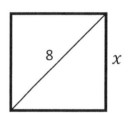

8) Choice B is correct

$Probability = \dfrac{number\ of\ desired\ outcomes}{number\ of\ total\ outcomes} = \dfrac{18}{12 + 18 + 18 + 24} = \dfrac{18}{72} = \dfrac{1}{4}$

9) Choice D is correct

$average = \dfrac{sum\ of\ terms}{number\ of\ terms} \Rightarrow$ (average of 6 numbers) $12 = \dfrac{sum\ of\ numbers}{6} \Rightarrow$ sum of 6 numbers is: $12 \times 6 = 72$

(average of 4 numbers) $10 = \dfrac{sum\ of\ numbers}{4} \Rightarrow$ sum of 4 numbers is $10 \times 4 = 40$

$sum\ of\ 6\ numbers - sum\ of\ 4\ numbers = sum\ of\ 2\ numbers$: $72 - 40 = 32$

average of 2 numbers $= \dfrac{32}{2} = 16$

10) Choice B is correct

The perimeter of the trapezoid is $36\ cm$. Therefore, the missing side (height) is:

$36 - 8 - 12 - 6 = 10$

Area of a trapezoid: $A = \frac{1}{2}h\ (b_1 + b_2) = \frac{1}{2}(10)(6 + 8) = 70$

11) Choice A is correct

Let x be the number of new shoes the team can purchase. Therefore, the team can purchase $120x$. The team had $20,000 and spent $14,000. Now the team can spend on new shoes $6,000 at most. Now, write the inequality: $120x + 14,000 \leq 20,000$

12) Choice B is correct

The probability of choosing a Hearts is $\frac{13}{52} = \frac{1}{4}$

13) Choice D is correct

First, find the sum of five numbers. $average = \frac{sum\ of\ terms}{number\ of\ terms} \Rightarrow 24 = \frac{sum\ of\ 5\ numbers}{5}$
$\Rightarrow sum\ of\ 5\ numbers = 24 \times 5 = 120$

The sum of 5 numbers is 120. If a sixth number that is greater than 42 is added to these numbers, then the sum of 6 numbers must be greater than 162.

$120 + 42 = 162$. If the number was 42, then the average of the numbers is:

$$average = \frac{sum\ of\ terms}{number\ of\ terms} = \frac{162}{6} = 27$$

Since the number is bigger than 42. Then, the average of six numbers must be greater than 27. Only Choice D is greater than 27.

14) Choice B is correct

The length of the rectangle is 24. Then, its width is 8. $24 \div 3 = 8$

$Perimeter\ of\ a\ rectangle = 2 \times width + 2 \times length = 2 \times 8 + 2 \times 24 = 16 + 48 = 64$

15) Choice D is correct

The ratio of oranges to apples is $3:8$. Therefore, there are 8 apples out of 11 fruits. To find the answer, write a proportion and solve for the unknown.

$\frac{8}{11} = \frac{x}{55} \Rightarrow x = \frac{8 \times 55}{11} = 40$. There are 40 apples in the basket.

16) Choice D is correct

Isolate and solve for x: $\frac{2}{3}x + \frac{1}{6} = \frac{1}{3} \Rightarrow \frac{2}{3}x = \frac{1}{3} - \frac{1}{6} = \frac{1}{6} \Rightarrow \frac{2}{3}x = \frac{1}{6}$

Multiply both sides by the reciprocal of the coefficient of x. $(\frac{3}{2})\frac{2}{3}x = \frac{1}{6}(\frac{3}{2}) \Rightarrow x = \frac{3}{12} = \frac{1}{4}$

17) Choice C is correct

$y = 2b^2 + 3ab + 3a^3$ Plug in the values of a and b in the equation: $a = 3$ and $b = 2$

$y = 2b^2 + 3ab + 3a^3 = 2(2)^2 + 3(3)(2) + 3(3)^3 = 2(4) + 3(3)(2) + 3(27) = 107$

18) Choice D is correct

Use Pythagorean Theorem: $a^2 + b^2 = c^2 \rightarrow 5^2 + 12^2 = c^2 \Rightarrow 169 = c^2 \Rightarrow c = 13$

19) Choice B is correct

Solve for x. $\frac{4x}{18} = \frac{x+1}{9}$. Multiply the second fraction by 2. $\frac{4x}{18} = \frac{2(x+1)}{2 \times 9}$. Two denominators are equal. Therefore, the numerators must be equal.

$4x = 2x + 2 \rightarrow 4x - 2x = 2 \rightarrow 2x = 2 \rightarrow x = \dfrac{2}{2} = 1$

20) Choice D is correct

To simplify this rational expression, combine the fractions in the denominator. Then:

$\dfrac{\frac{1}{3} - \frac{x+6}{6}}{\frac{x^2}{2} - \frac{4}{2}} = \dfrac{\frac{1}{3} - \frac{x+6}{6}}{\frac{x^2-4}{2}}$, now simplify the fractions in the numerator: $\dfrac{\frac{1}{3} - \frac{x+6}{6}}{\frac{x^2}{2} - \frac{4}{2}} = \dfrac{\frac{1}{3} - \frac{x+6}{6}}{\frac{x^2-4}{2}} = \dfrac{\frac{2-x-6}{6}}{\frac{x^2-4}{2}}$

Apply this fraction rule: $\dfrac{\frac{a}{b}}{\frac{c}{d}} \rightarrow \dfrac{a \times d}{b \times c}$. Then: $\dfrac{\frac{-x-4}{6}}{\frac{x^2-4}{2}} = \dfrac{2(-x-4)}{6(x^2-4)} = \dfrac{-2x-8}{6x^2-24}$, divide both numerator and denominator by 2. Then: $\dfrac{-2x-8}{6x^2-24} = \dfrac{-x-4}{3x^2-12}$

Accuplacer Mathematics Practice Test 2

Advanced Algebra and Functions

1) Choice D is correct

Since $N = 6$, substitute 6 for N in the equation $\frac{x-3}{5} = N$, which gives $\frac{x-3}{5} = 6$. Multiplying both sides of $\frac{x-3}{5} = 6$ by 5 gives $x - 3 = 30$ and then adding 3 to both sides of $x - 3 = 30$ then, $x = 33$.

2) Choice C is correct

$b^{\frac{m}{n}} = \sqrt[n]{b^m}$, for any positive integers m and n. Thus, $b^{\frac{3}{5}} = \sqrt[5]{b^3}$.

3) Choice B is correct

The total number of pages read by Sara is 3 (hours she spent reading) multiplied by her rate of reading: $\frac{N \, pages}{hour} \times 3 \, hours = 3N$

Similarly, the total number of pages read by Mary is 4 (hours she spent reading) multiplied by her rate of reading: $\frac{M \, pages}{hour} \times 4 \, hours = 4M$ the total number of pages read by Sara and Mary is the sum of the total number of pages read by Sara and the total number of pages read by Mary: $3N + 4M$.

4) Choice C is correct

We know that: $i = \sqrt{-1} \Rightarrow i^2 = -1$, $(-4 + 9i)(3 + 5i) = -12 - 20i + 27i + 45i^2 = -12 + 7i - 45 = -57 + 7i$

5) Choice C is correct

First find the value of b, and then find $f(5)$. Since $f(2) = 35$, substuting 2 for x and 35 for $f(x)$ gives $35 = b(2)^2 + 15 = 4b + 15$. Solving this equation gives $b = 5$. Thus

$f(x) = 5x^2 + 15$, $f(5) = 5(5)^2 + 15 \rightarrow f(5) = 125 + 15 = 140$

6) Choice D is correct

Solving Systems of Equations by Elimination: Multiply the first equation by (-2), then add it to the second equation.

$$\begin{array}{l} -2(2x + 5y = 11) \\ \underline{4x - 2y = -14} \end{array} \Rightarrow \begin{array}{l} -4x - 10y = -22 \\ \underline{4x - 2y = -14} \end{array} \Rightarrow -12y = -36 \Rightarrow y = 3$$

Plug in the value of y into one of the equations and solve for x.

$2x + 5(3) = 11 \Rightarrow 2x + 15 = 11 \Rightarrow 2x = -4 \Rightarrow x = -2$

7) Choice A is correct

Identify the input value. Since the function is in the form $f(x)$ and the question asks to calculate $f(4)$, the input value is four. $f(4) \rightarrow x = 4$, Using the function, input the desired x value. Now substitute 4 in for every x in the function. $f(x) = 3x^2 - 4 \Rightarrow$

$f(4) = 3(4)^2 - 4 \Rightarrow f(4) = 48 - 4 \Rightarrow f(4) = 44$

8) Choice D is correct

Frist factor the function: $f(x) = x^3 + 5x^2 + 6x = x (x + 2)(x + 3)$, To find the zeros, $f(x)$ should be zero. $f(x) = x (x + 2)(x + 3) = 0$, Therefore, the zeros are: $x = 0$, $(x + 2) = 0 \Rightarrow$ $x = -2$, $(x + 3) = 0 \Rightarrow x = -3$

9) Choice D is correct

Recall that the imaginary numbers (contain i) cannot be in the denominator of a fraction. To simplify the expression, multiply both numerator and denominator by i.

$\frac{4-3i}{-4i} \times \frac{i}{i} = \frac{4i-3i^2}{-4i^2}$, $i^2 - 1$, Then: $\frac{4i-3i^2}{-4i^2} = \frac{4i-3(-1)}{-4(-1)} = \frac{4i+3}{4} = \frac{4i}{4} + \frac{3}{4} = \frac{3}{4} + i$

10) Choice D is correct

The x-intercepts of the parabola represented by $y = x^2 - 7x + 12$ in the xy-plane are the values of x for which y is equal to 0. The factored form of the equation,

$y = (x - 3)(x - 4)$, shows that y equals 0 if and only if $x = 3$ or $x = 4$. Thus, the factored form $y = (x - 3)(x - 4)$, displays the x-intercepts of the parabola as the constants 3 and 4.

11) Choice C is correct

If $x - a$ is a factor of $g(x)$, then $g(a)$ must equal 0. Based on the table

$g(2) = 0$. Therefore, $x - 2$ must be a factor of $g(x)$.

12) Choice C is correct

To solve this problem first solve the equation for . $\frac{c}{b} = 2$, Multiply by b on both sides. Then: $b \times \frac{c}{b} = 2 \times b \rightarrow c = 2b$. Now to calculate $\frac{4b}{c}$, substitute the value for c into the denominator and simplify. $\frac{4b}{c} = \frac{4b}{2b} = \frac{4}{2} = \frac{2}{1} = 2$

13) Choice B is correct

$x + 5 = 8 \rightarrow x = 8 - 5 = 3$, and $2y - 1 = 5 \rightarrow 2y = 6 \rightarrow y = 3$, Then:

$xy + 15 = 3 \times 3 + 15 = 24$

14) Choice B is correct

The equation $\frac{a-b}{b} = \frac{10}{13}$ can be rewritten as $\frac{a}{b} - \frac{b}{b} = \frac{10}{13}$, from which it follows that

$\frac{a}{b} - 1 = \frac{10}{13}$, or $\frac{a}{b} = \frac{10}{13} + 1 = \frac{23}{13}$.

15) Choice A is correct

First write the equation in slope intercept form. Add $2x$ to both sides to get

$6y = 2x + 24$. Now divide both sides by 6 to get $y = \frac{1}{3}x + 4$. The slope of this line is $\frac{1}{3}$,

so any line that also has a slope of $\frac{1}{3}$ would be parallel to it. Only choice A has a slope

of $\frac{1}{3}$.

16) Choice D is correct

$average = \dfrac{sum\ of\ terms}{number\ of\ terms} \Rightarrow 20 = \dfrac{13 + 15 + 20 + x}{4} \Rightarrow 80 = 48 + x \Rightarrow x = 32$

17) Choice B is correct

The two angles are complementary angles (their sum is 90 degrees). Then:

$(x - 10) + (2x + 1) = 90 \rightarrow 3x - 9 = 90 \rightarrow 3x = 99 \rightarrow x = 33$.

18) Choice A is correct

The sum of all angles in a quadrilateral is 360 degrees. Let x be the smallest angle in the quadrilateral. Then the angles are: $x, 2x, 3x, 4x$. Then: $x + 2x + 3x + 4x = 360 \rightarrow 10x = 360 \rightarrow x = 36$, The angles in the quadrilateral are: $36°, 72°, 108°$, and $144°$. The smallest angle is 36 degrees.

19) Choice A is correct

Since a box of pen costs $3, then $3p$ represents the cost of p boxes of pen. Multiplying this number times 1.085 will increase the cost by the 8.5% for tax. Then add the $6 shipping fee for the total: $1.085(3p) + 6$

20) Choice D is correct

Rate of change (growth or x) is 8 per week. $40 \div 5 = 8$, Since the plant grows at a linear rate, then the relationship between the height (y) of the plant and number of weeks of growth (x) can be written as: $y(x) = 8x$

ACCUPLACER Mathematics Practice Test 3

Arithmetic

1) Choice D is correct

To compare fractions, find a common denominator. When two fractions have common denominators, the fraction with the larger numerator is the larger number. Choice A is incorrect because $\frac{3}{4}$ is not less than $\frac{17}{24}$. Write both fractions with common denominator and compare the numerators. $\frac{3}{4} = \frac{18}{24}$. The fraction $\frac{18}{24}$ is greater than $\frac{17}{24}$.

Choice B and C are not correct. Shown written with a common denominator, the comparisons $\frac{2}{3} < \frac{5}{9}$ and $\frac{3}{8} < \frac{9}{25}$ are not correct. Shown written with a common denominator, the comparison $\frac{11}{21} < \frac{4}{7}$ is correct because $\frac{4}{7}$ or $\frac{12}{21}$ is greater than $\frac{11}{21}$.

2) Choice A is correct

First multiply the tenths place of 7.8 by 4.56. The result is 3.648. Next, multiply 7 by 4.56 which results in 31.92. The sum of these two numbers is: $3.648 + 31.92 = 35.568$

3) Choice D is correct

Dividing 72 by 12%, which is equivalent to 0.12, gives 600. Therefore, 12% of 600 is 72.

4) Choice B is correct.

$\frac{13}{8} = 1.625$, the only choice that is greater than 1.625 is $\frac{5}{2}$.

$\frac{5}{2} = 2.5, 2.5 > 1.6$

5) Choice D is correct

The result when 879 is divided by 9 is 97 with a remainder of 6. Multiplying $9 \times 97 = 873$ and $879 - 873 = 6$, which is the remainder.

6) Choice C is correct

$2,782.5 \times 0.0001 = 2,782.5 \times \frac{1}{10,000} = 0.27825$

7) Choice D is correct

$2.5\% \; of \; 650 = 0.025 \times 650 = 16.25$. From the choices provided, choice D is correct. $\frac{65}{4} = 16.25$

8) Choice A is correct

$$\frac{6}{20} + \frac{1}{80} = \frac{24}{80} + \frac{1}{80} = \frac{25}{80} = \frac{5}{16}$$

9) Choice D is correct

$\frac{6}{3} \div \frac{1}{4} = \frac{6}{3} \times 4 = 8$. The number 8 is between 7 and 9.

10) Choice B is correct

The formula to find Percent of Change is $\frac{New\ Value - Old\ Value}{Old\ Value} \times 100\%$, so for our athlete, our new weight is 165 pounds and the original weight is 200 pounds.

$\frac{165 - 200}{200} \times 100\% = -17.5\%$.

11) Choice C is correct

$-4(8 \div 2)^2 = (-4) \times (8 \div 2)^2 = (-4) \times (4)^2 = (-4) \times (16) = -64$

12) Choice D is correct

First simplify the multiplication: $\frac{5}{4} \times \frac{6}{2} = \frac{30}{8} = \frac{15}{4}$, Choice D is equal to $\frac{15}{4}$.

$\frac{5 \times 3}{4} = \frac{15}{4}$

13) Choice C is correct

$\frac{35}{20} = 1.75$, converting 1.75 to percent we have: $1.75 = 175\%$. Then, 35 is 175% of 20.

14) Choice B is correct

To add decimal numbers, line them up and add from right.

$3.85 + 0.045 + 0.1365 = 4.0315$

15) Choice C is correct

$(-2)^3 + (-4)^2 = (-2)(-2)(-2) + (-4)(-4) = -8 + 16 = 8$

16) Choice B is correct

Let's compare the fractions: $\frac{7}{8} > \frac{9}{11} > \frac{2}{3} > \frac{3}{5}$, only choice B provides the right order.

17) Choice C is correct

$\frac{2}{4} + \frac{3}{2} - \frac{1}{4} = \frac{2 + 6 - 1}{4} = \frac{7}{4} = 1.75$

18) Choice B is correct

$\frac{(8 + 6)^2}{2} + 6 = \frac{(14)^2}{2} + 6 = \frac{196}{2} + 6 = 98 + 6 = 104$

19)Choice C is correct

The remaining length of cable: $400 - 20 = 380$, let x be the weight of the remaining cable. Then: $\frac{x}{380} = \frac{80}{400} \Rightarrow 400x = 380 \times 80 \Rightarrow 400x = 30,400 \Rightarrow x = \frac{30,400}{400} = 76$

The weight of the remaining cable is 76 pounds.

20)Choice D is correct

78 divided by 5, the remainder is 3. 45 divided by 7, the remainder is also 3.

Accuplacer Mathematics Practice Test 3

Quantitative Reasoning, Algebra, and Statistics

1) Choice C is correct

Using rules of exponents, start in the numerator $(-2x^2y^2)^3$ is $(-2)^3 (x^2)^3(y^2)^3$ which simplifies to $-8x^6y^6$. That is multiplied by $3x^3y$ giving $-24x^9y^7$. Next, divide $\frac{-24x^9y^7}{12x^3y^8}$ to get $\frac{-2x^6}{y}$.

2) Choice D is correct

Start by using the distributive property to simplify the left side of the inequality and combining like terms to get $-2x - 8 \geq x + 6$. To isolate x, subtract x and add 8 to both sides. This gives $-3x \geq 14$. To isolate the x, divide both sides by -3. Dividing by the negative changes the relationship between the sides and gives $x \leq -\frac{14}{3}$.

3) Choice C is correct

The expression 4^{-3} can be rewritten as $\frac{1}{4^3}$, which is equal to: $\frac{1}{4\times4\times4} = \frac{1}{64}$

4) Choice C is correct

The formula for factoring the difference of two cubes is:

$(a^3 - b^3) = (a - b)(a^2 + ab + b^2)$. Here $x^3 - 8 = x^3 - 2^3$. Replacing a with x and b with 2 gives: $(x - 2)(x^2 + 2x + 4)$

5) Choice C is correct

The value of $g(15)$ can be found by substituting 15 for x in the equation for $g(x)$. This yield $g(15) = 5(15 - 6)$, which equivalent to $5 \times (9)$ or 45.

6) Choice A is correct

The formula for the area of a circle is: $A = \pi r^2$. Using 49 for the area of the circle we have: $49 = \pi r^2$. Let's solve for the radius (r). $\frac{49}{\pi} = r^2 \rightarrow r = \sqrt{\frac{49}{\pi}} = \frac{7}{\sqrt{\pi}} = \frac{7}{\sqrt{\pi}} \times \frac{\sqrt{\pi}}{\sqrt{\pi}} = \frac{7\sqrt{\pi}}{\pi}$

7) Choice D is correct

First, distribute the d to get $N = s + ad - d$, next isolate the term with the a by subtracting s from both sides and adding d to both sides to get $N - s + d = ad$. Divide both sides by d to get: $a = \frac{N-s+d}{d}$.

8) Choice C is correct

The relationship among all sides of special right triangle

$30° - 60° - 90°$ is provided in this triangle:

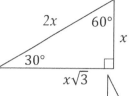

In this triangle, the opposite side of $30°$ angle is half of the hypotenuse.

Draw the shape of this question: The ladder is the hypotenuse.

Therefore, the ladder is $70 \ ft$.

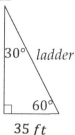

9) Choice C is correct

Use Pythagorean theorem to find the value of y: $a^2 + b^2 = c^2 \rightarrow 3^2 + 4^2 = y^2 \rightarrow$

$y^2 = 9 + 16 = 25 \rightarrow y = 5$. The perimeter of the trapezoid is: $8 + 3 + 5 + 8 + 4 = 28$ (notice that $x = 4$).

10) Choice D is correct

First find the slope of the line using the slope formula: $m = \frac{y_2 - y_1}{x_2 - x_1}$, Substituting in the known information. $(x_1, y_1) = (4, 3)$, $(x_2, y_2) = (3, 2)$, $m = \frac{2-3}{3-4} = \frac{-1}{-1} = 1$

Now use the slope to find the equation of the line passing through these points.

$y = mx + b$, Choose one of the points and plug in the values of x and y in the equation to solve for b. Let's choose point $(4, 3)$. Then: $y = mx + b \rightarrow 3 = 1(4) + b \rightarrow 3 = 4 + b \rightarrow$

$y = mx + b \rightarrow 3 = 1(4) + b \rightarrow 3 = 4 + b \rightarrow b = 3 - 4 = -1$

The equation of the line is: $y = x - 1$

Now, plug in the points provided in the choices into the equation of the line.

A. $(-1, 2)$ $y = x - 1 \rightarrow 2 = (-1) - 1 \rightarrow 2 \neq -2$ This is NOT true.

B. $(5, 7)$ $y = x - 1 \rightarrow 7 = (5) - 1 \rightarrow 7 \neq 4$ This is NOT true.

C. $(3, 4)$ $y = x - 1 \rightarrow 4 = (3) - 1 \rightarrow 4 \neq 2$ This is NOT true.

D. $(-1, -2)$ $y = x - 1 \rightarrow -2 = (-1) - 1 \rightarrow -2 = -2$ This is true!

Therefore, the only point from the choices that on the line is $(-1, -2)$.

11) Choice C is correct

Let x be the number. Write the equation and solve for x.

$\frac{3}{5} \times 20 = \frac{3}{4}x \rightarrow \frac{3 \times 20}{5} = \frac{3x}{4}$, use cross multiplication to solve for x.

$4 \times 60 = 3x \times 5 \rightarrow 240 = 15x \rightarrow x = 16$

12)Choice B is correct

$3f = 3 \times (3x + 2y) = 9x + 6y,\ 3f + g = 9x + 6y + x - 5y = 10x + y$

13)Choice C is correct.

The speed of train B is: $\frac{500}{5} = 100\ km/h$. Then, the speed of train A is: $\frac{6}{5} \times 100 = 120\ km/h$

14)Choice B is correct

If the score of James was 90, therefore the score of Robert is 30. Since the score of David was half as that of Robert, therefore, the score of David is 15.

15)Choice C is correct

The rate of construction company $= \frac{40\ cm}{1\ min} = 40\frac{cm}{min}$. The height of the wall after $50\ min = \frac{40\ cm}{1\ min} \times 50\ min = 2,000\ cm$. Let x be the height of wall, then $\frac{2}{3}x = 2,000\ cm \rightarrow$

$$x = \frac{3 \times 2,000}{2} \rightarrow x = 3,000\ cm = 30\ m$$

16)Choice B is correct

There are several ways to graph a line. For this one, it is convenient to find the x intercept and the y intercept. To find the x intercept, substitute 0 for y, resulting is the equation $4x = 8$. Dividing both sides by 4, gives $x = 2$. Plot the point $(2, 0)$. To find the y intercept, substitute 0 for x, resulting is the equation $2y = 8$. Dividing both sides by 2, gives $y = 4$. Plot the point $(0, 4)$. Drawing the line through the two points gives the graph in B.

17)Choice B is correct

Let x be the minimum score on Robert's 4th test. Then:

$$average = \frac{sum\ of\ terms}{number\ of\ terms} \Rightarrow 90 = \frac{89 + 76 + 98 + x}{4} \Rightarrow 90 = \frac{263 + x}{4} \Rightarrow$$

$360 = 263 + x \Rightarrow x = 360 - 263 \Rightarrow x = 97$

18)Choice B is correct

Write the numbers in order: $2, 3, 5, 8, 10, 12, 15, 19$. Since we have 8 numbers (8 is even), then the median is $(8 + 10) \div 2 = 9$.

19) Choice D is correct

Formula for the surface area of a cylinder is:

$SA = 2\pi r^2 + 2\pi rh \rightarrow 150\pi = 2\pi r^2 + 2\pi r(10)$

Both sides divided by 2π: $\rightarrow r^2 + 10r - 75 = 0$

$(r + 15)(r - 5) = 0 \rightarrow r = 5 \ or \ r = -15 \ (unacceptable)$

20) Choice A is correct

James starts off with \$80, and spends \$4.5 every day. This means that he will have \$75.5 after day 1, \$71 after day 2, and so forth. Only one equation satisfies this scenario. The rest are irrelevant. $T = 80 - 4.5D$

Accuplacer Mathematics Practice Test 3

Advanced Algebra and Functions

1) Choice C is correct

Plugin the values of x and y provided in the choices into both equations.

Let's start with $x + y = 0$

A. $(4,3)$ $x + y = 0 \rightarrow 4 + 3 \neq 0$

B. $(5,4)$ $x + y = 0 \rightarrow 5 + 4 \neq 0$

C. $(4,-4)$ $x + y = 0 \rightarrow 4 + (-4) = 0$

D. $(4,-6)$ $x + y = 0 \rightarrow 4 + (-6) \neq 0$

2) Choice A is correct

If $f(x) = 3x + 4(x + 1) + 2$, then find $f(3x)$ by substituting $3x$ for every x in the function. This gives: $f(3x) = 3(3x) + 4(3x + 1) + 2$

It simplifies to: $f(3x) = 3(3x) + 4(3x + 1) + 2 = 9x + 12x + 4 + 2 = 21x + 6$.

3) Choice D is correct

Perfect square formula: $(a - b)^2 = a^2 - 2ab + b^2$. So, $(5x - 3y)^2 =$

$25x^2 - 30xy + 9y^2 = 25x^2 + 9y^2 - 30xy$

4) Choice C is correct

$(3n^2 + 4n + 6) - (2n^2 - 5)$. Add like terms together: $3n^2 - 2n^2 = n^2$

$4n$ doesn't have like terms. $6 - (-5) = 11$

Combine these terms into one expression to find the answer: $n^2 + 4n + 11$

5) Choice C is correct

You can find the possible values of a and b in $(ax + 4)(bx + 3)$ by using the given equation $a + b = 7$ and finding another equation that relates the variables a and b. Since $(ax + 4)(bx + 3) = 10x^2 + cx + 12$, expand the left side of the equation to obtain $abx^2 + 4bx + 3ax + 12 = 10x^2 + cx + 12$. Since ab is the coefficient of x^2 on the left side of the equation and 10 is the coefficient of x^2 on the right side of the equation, it must be true that $ab = 10$. The coefficient of x on the left side is $4b + 3a$ and the coefficient of x in the right side is c. Then: $4b + 3a = c$, $a + b = 7$, then: $a = 7 - b$. Now, plug in the value of a in the equation $ab = 10$. Then: $ab = 10 \rightarrow (7 - b)b = 10 \rightarrow 7b - b^2 = 10$. Add $-7b + b^2$ to both sides. Then: $b^2 - 7b + 10 = 0$. Solve for b using the

factoring method. $b^2 - 7b + 10 = 0 \rightarrow (b-5)(b-2) = 0$. Thus, either $b = 2$ and $a = 5$, or $b = 5$ and $a = 2$. If $b = 2$ and $a = 5$, then $4b + 3a = c \rightarrow 4(2) + 3(5) = c \rightarrow c = 23$. If $b = 5$ and $a = 2$, then, $4b + 3a = c \rightarrow 4(5) + 3(2) = c \rightarrow c = 26$. Therefore, the two possible values for c are 23 and 26.

6) Choice A is correct

To rewrite $\dfrac{1}{\frac{1}{x-6}+\frac{1}{x+4}}$, first simplify $\dfrac{1}{x-6} + \dfrac{1}{x+4}$

$$\frac{1}{x-6} + \frac{1}{x+4} = \frac{1(x+4)}{(x-6)(x+4)} + \frac{1(x-6)}{(x+4)(x-6)} = \frac{(x+4)+(x-6)}{(x+4)(x-6)}$$

Then: $\dfrac{1}{\frac{1}{x-6}+\frac{1}{x+4}} = \dfrac{1}{\frac{(x+4)+(x-6)}{(x+4)(x-6)}} = \dfrac{(x-6)(x+4)}{(x-6)+(x+4)}$. (Remember, $\dfrac{1}{\frac{1}{x}} = x$)

This result is equivalent to the expression in choice A.

7) Choice C is correct

The range of a function describes set all outputs, y, that satisfy the equation defining the function. In the $xy-$plan, the graph of $y = -3x^4 + 6$ is a U-shaped graph that opens downward with its vertex at $(0, 6)$. Because the graph opens downward, the vertex indicates the maximum value of y is 6. Therefore, the range of the function defined by $y = -3x^4 + 6$ is the set of $y-$values less than or equal to 6.

8) Choice D is correct

First find the slope of the line using the slope formula. $m = \dfrac{y_2 - y_1}{x_2 - x_1}$

Substituting in the known information. $(x_1, y_1) = (2, 4)$, $(x_2, y_2) = (4, 5)$

$m = \dfrac{5-4}{4-2} = \dfrac{1}{2}$. Now use the slope to find the equation of the line passing through these points. Choose one of the points and plug in the values of x and y in the equation to solve for b. Let's choose point $(4, 5)$. Then: $y = mx + b \rightarrow 5 = \dfrac{1}{2}(4) + b \rightarrow 5 = 2 + b \rightarrow b = 5 - 2 = 3$

The equation of the line is: $y = \dfrac{1}{2}x + 3$

Now, plug in the points provided in the choices into the equation of the line.

A. $(9, 9)$ $\qquad$ $y = \dfrac{1}{2}x + 3 \rightarrow 9 = \dfrac{1}{2}(9) + 3 \rightarrow 9 \neq 7.5$ This is NOT true.

B. $(9, 6)$ $\qquad$ $y = \dfrac{1}{2}x + 3 \rightarrow 6 = \dfrac{1}{2}(9) + 3 \rightarrow 6 \neq 7.5$ This is NOT true.

C. $(6, 9)$ $\qquad$ $y = \dfrac{1}{2}x + 3 \rightarrow 9 = \dfrac{1}{2}(6) + 3 \rightarrow 9 \neq 6$ $\quad$ This is NOT true.

D. $(6,6)$ $y = \frac{1}{2}x + 3 \rightarrow 6 = \frac{1}{2}(6) + 3 \rightarrow 6 = 6$ This is true!

Therefore, the only point from the choices that lies on the line is $(6,6)$.

9) Choice B is correct

The input value is 4. Then: $x = 4$

$f(x) = x^2 - 3x \rightarrow f(4) = 4^2 - 3(4) = 16 - 12 = 4$

10) Choice D is correct

Remember that in the equation of a line: $y = mx + b$, Where $m = slope$, $y - intercept$ is given by b. Let's review the choices.

A. $y = -3x + 5$ has a $y - intercept$ at $(0,5)$

B. $y = 4x + 7$ has a $y - intercept$ at $(0,7)$

C. $y = 5 + 4x$ has a $y - intercept$ at $(0,5)$

D. $y = 4 - x$ has a $y - intercept$ at $(0,4)$, so this is the correct answer

11) Choice C is correct

Multiplying each side of $\frac{3}{x} = \frac{12}{x-9}$ by $x(x-9)$ gives $3(x-9) = 12(x)$, distributing the 3 over the values within the parentheses yields $x - 9 = 4x$ or $x = -3$.

Therefore, the value of $\frac{x}{6} = \frac{-3}{6} = -\frac{1}{2}$.

12) Choice D is correct

The equation of a circle can be written as $(x - h)^2 + (y - k)^2 = r^2$, where (h, k) are the coordinates of the center of the circle and r is the radius of the circle. Since the coordinates of the center of the circle are $(0,4)$, the equation is $x^2 + (y - 4)^2 = r^2$, where r is the radius. The radius of the circle is the distance from the center $(0,4)$, to the given endpoint of a radius, $\left(\frac{5}{3}, 6\right)$. By the distance formula,

$r^2 = \left(\frac{5}{3} - 0\right)^2 + (6 - 4)^2 = \frac{61}{9}$. Therefore, an equation of the given circle is:

$x^2 + (y - 4)^2 = \frac{61}{9}$

13) Choice C is correct

To solve for $\cos A$, first identify what is known. The question states that ΔABC is a right triangle whose $n\angle B = 90°$ and $\sin C = \frac{2}{3}$. It is important to recall that any triangle has a sum of interior angles that equals 180 degrees. Therefore, to calculate $\cos A$ use the complimentary angles identify of trigonometric function. $\cos A = \cos(90 - C)$,

Then: $\cos A = \sin C$. For complementary angles, $\sin$ of one angle is equal to $\cos$ of the other angle. $\cos A = \frac{2}{3}$

14) Choice C is correct

The general form of absolute function is: $f(x) = a|x - h| + k$

Since the graph opens downward with a slope of 1, then a is negative one. The graph moved 1 unit up, so the value of k is 1. Then, choice C is correct. $y = -|x| + 1$

15) Choice C is correct

The line passes through the origin, $(6, m)$ and $(m, 12)$. Any two of these points can be used to find the slope of the line. Since the line passes through $(0, 0)$ and $(6, m)$, the slope of the line is equal to $\frac{m-0}{6-0} = \frac{m}{6}$. Similarly, since the line passes through $(0, 0)$ and $(m, 12)$, the slope of the line is equal to $\frac{12-0}{m-0} = \frac{12}{m}$. Since each expression gives the slope of the same line, it must be true that $\frac{m}{6} = \frac{12}{m}$. Using cross multiplication gives

$$\frac{m}{6} = \frac{12}{m} \rightarrow m^2 = 72 \rightarrow m = \pm\sqrt{72} = \pm\sqrt{36 \times 2} = \pm\sqrt{36} \times \sqrt{2} = \pm 6\sqrt{2}$$

16) Choice B is correct

It is given that $g(6) = 4$. Then: $f(g(6)) = f(4) = 7$

17) Choice A is correct

By definition, area of the equilateral triangle is: $\frac{\sqrt{3}\,d^2}{4}$

You can also find the height of the triangle using the relationship in $30° - 60° - 90°$ triangles. The relationship among all sides of special right triangle $30° - 60° - 90°$ is provided in this triangle:

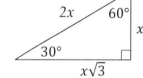

In the equilateral triangle the side is d. Then, $2x = d \rightarrow x = \frac{d}{2}$

The height of the triangle is: $\frac{d}{2} \times \sqrt{3} = \frac{d\sqrt{3}}{2}$. Then, the area of the triangle is: $\frac{1}{2}(d)\left(\frac{d\sqrt{3}}{2}\right) = \frac{\sqrt{3}\,d^2}{4}$

18) Choice A is correct

Subtract the area of the circle from the area of the square and divide the result by 4. The side of the square is equal to the diameter of the circle, so each side is equal to 8.

Area of the square $\rightarrow 8 \times 8 = 64$. Area of the circle $\rightarrow A = \pi r^2 = (4 \times 4)\pi = 16\pi$

Area of the shaded region $\rightarrow \frac{64-16\pi}{4} = \frac{64}{4} - \frac{16\pi}{4} = 16 - 4\pi$

19)Choice C is correct

The equation of a circle in standard form is: $(x - h)^2 + (y - k)^2 = r^2$, where r is the radius of the circle. In this circle the radius is 4.

$r^2 = 16 \rightarrow r = 4, (x + 2)^2 + (y - 4)^2 = 16.$ Area of a circle: $A = \pi r^2 = \pi(4)^2 = 16\pi$

20)Choice B is correct

By definition, the sine of any acute angle is equal to the cosine of its complement. Since, angle A and B are complementary angles, therefore: $\sin A = \cos B$

ACCUPLACER Mathematical Reasoning Practice Test 4

Arithmetic

1) Choice B is correct

5 percent of $560 = \dfrac{5}{100} \times 560 = \dfrac{1}{20} \times 560 = \dfrac{560}{20} = 28$

2) Choice C is correct

A. $\dfrac{3}{5} > \dfrac{2}{3} \rightarrow \dfrac{9}{15} > \dfrac{10}{15}$ This is NOT true.

B. $\dfrac{3}{7} < \dfrac{2}{5} \rightarrow \dfrac{15}{35} < \dfrac{14}{35}$ This is NOT true.

C. $\dfrac{5}{8} > \dfrac{6}{10} \rightarrow \dfrac{50}{80} > \dfrac{48}{80}$ This is TRUE.

D. $\dfrac{4}{7} > \dfrac{6}{9} \rightarrow \dfrac{36}{63} > \dfrac{42}{63}$ This is NOT true.

3) Choice D is correct.

$75 off is the same as 20 percent off. Thus, 20 percent of a number is 75.

Then: $20\% \ of \ x = 75 \rightarrow 0.2x = 75 \rightarrow x = \dfrac{75}{0.2} = 375$

4) Choice C is correct

To find 25% of $130.00, multiply $130.00 by 0.25, which is $32.50. Choice B is correct because $32.50 is 25% of $130.

5) Choice A is correct

$\dfrac{1\frac{5}{4} + \frac{1}{3}}{2\frac{1}{2} - \frac{15}{8}} = \dfrac{\frac{9}{4} + \frac{1}{3}}{\frac{5}{2} - \frac{15}{8}} = \dfrac{\frac{27+4}{12}}{\frac{20-15}{8}} = \dfrac{\frac{31}{12}}{\frac{5}{8}} = \dfrac{31 \times 8}{12 \times 5} = \dfrac{31 \times 2}{3 \times 5} = \dfrac{62}{15} \approx 4.133$

6) Choice A is correct

To find the sum of three whole numbers, line the numbers up and add digits from right.

$$\begin{array}{r} 1.578 \\ + \ 11.104 \\ + \ \ 0.017 \\ \hline 12.699 \end{array}$$

7) Choice D is correct

First multiply the tenths place of 3.6 by 9.85. The result is 5.91. Next, multiply 3 by 9.85 which results in 29.55. The sum of these two numbers is: $5.91 + 29.55 = 35.46$

8) Choice A is correct

First, find the number. Let x be the number. 80% of a number is 400, then:

$0.8 \times x = 400 \Rightarrow x = 400 \div 0.8 = 500$. 40% of 500 is: $0.4 \times 500 = 200$

9) Choice C is correct

The result when 754 is divided by 7 is 107 with a remainder of 5. Multiplying $7 \times 107 = 749$ and $754 - 749 = 5$, which is the remainder.

10) Choice A is correct

$\frac{3}{2} = 1.5$. The only choice less than 1.5 is 1.3. $\frac{3}{2} = 1.5 > 1.3$

11) Choice A is correct

Find the sum of five numbers. $average = \frac{sum\ of\ terms}{number\ of\ terms} \Rightarrow 37 = \frac{sum\ of\ 5\ numbers}{5} \Rightarrow$ $sum\ of\ 5\ numbers = 37 \times 5 = 185$. The sum of 5 numbers is 185. If a sixth number 43 is added, then the sum of 6 numbers is $185 + 43 = 228$. The new average is: $\frac{sum\ of\ 6\ numbers}{6} = \frac{228}{6} = 38$

12) Choice D is correct

Dividing 75 by 15%, which is equivalent to 0.15, gives 500.

13) Choice C is correct

The pass rate is 18 out of $45 = \frac{18}{45}$. Change the fraction to percent: $\frac{18}{45} \times 100\% = 40\%$

40 percent of drivers passed. Therefore, 60 percent of drivers failed the test.

14) Choice B is correct

Use simple interest formula: $I = prt$ (I = interest, p = principal, r = rate, t = time)

$I = (2,500)(0.03)(3) = 225$

15) Choice B is correct

$\frac{8}{2} \div \frac{4}{7} = \frac{8}{2} \times \frac{7}{4} = \frac{56}{8} = 7$

16) Choice D is correct

Let's review the choices provided.

A: $\frac{1}{9} = 0.111$, B: $\frac{9}{10} = 0.9$, C: $\frac{9}{100} = 0.09$, D: $\frac{9}{1,000} = 0.009$. So, choice D is correct.

17) Choice D is correct

The amount of money that Jack earns for one hour: $\frac{\$616}{44} = \$14$

Number of additional hours that he needs to work to make enough money is:

$\frac{\$826 - \$616}{1.5 \times \$14} = 10$. Number of total hours is: $44 + 10 = 54$

18) Choice B is correct

$1\frac{2}{3} + 2\frac{1}{6} - 2\frac{1}{3} - 1\frac{1}{6} = \frac{5}{3} + \frac{13}{6} - \frac{7}{3} - \frac{7}{6} = \frac{10 + 13 - 14 - 7}{6} = \frac{2}{6} = \frac{1}{3}$.

19) Choice D is correct

To compare the numbers, they should be put in the same format. The percent 37% can be converted to a decimal by dividing 37 by 100, which gives 0.37. $\frac{3}{8}$ can be converted to a decimal by dividing 3 by 8, which gives 0.375. $\frac{2}{5}$ can be converted to a decimal by dividing 2 by 5, which gives 0.4. $\frac{9}{20}$ can be converted to a decimal by dividing 9 by 20, which gives 0.45. Now, all three numbers are in decimal format. $0.45 > 0.4 > 0.375 > 0.37 > 0.0375$ or $\frac{9}{20}, \frac{2}{5}, \frac{3}{8}, 37\%, 0.0375$, which is choice D.

20) Choice C is correct

The fraction $\frac{3}{5}$ can be written as $\frac{3 \times 20}{5 \times 20} = \frac{60}{100}$, which can be interpreted as sixty hundredths, or 0.60.

Accuplacer Mathematics Practice Test 4

Quantitative Reasoning, Algebra, And Statistics

1) Choice C is correct

Red and blue balls are in ratio of $2:3$. Write a proportion and solve.

$\frac{2}{3} = \frac{x}{75} \rightarrow 3x = 2 \times 75 \rightarrow 3x = 150 \rightarrow x = \frac{150}{3} = 50$

2) Choice A is correct

Plug in the values of x and y from choices provided.

A. $(-2, 3)$	$x + 2y = 4 \rightarrow -2 + 2(3) = 4 \rightarrow -2 + 6 = 4$	This is true!
B. $(1, 2)$	$x + 2y = 4 \rightarrow 1 + 2(2) = 4 \rightarrow 1 + 4 \neq 4$	This is NOT true!
C. $(-1, 3)$	$x + 2y = 4 \rightarrow -1 + 2(3) = 4 \rightarrow -1 + 6 \neq 4$	This is NOT true!
D. $(-3, 4)$	$x + 2y = 4 \rightarrow -3 + 2(4) = 4 \rightarrow -3 + 8 \neq 4$	This is NOT true!

3) Choice B is correct

The length of the rectangle is: $\frac{3}{2} \times 30 = 45 \ cm$. The perimeter of rectangle is:

$2 \times (length + width) = 2 \times (30 + 45) = 150 \ cm$

4) Choice C is correct

To solve for the variable, isolate it on one side of the equation. For this equation, multiply both sides by 5. Then: $\frac{3x}{5} = 27 \rightarrow \frac{3x}{5} \times 5 = 27 \times 5 \rightarrow 3x = 135$

Now, divide both sides by 3. $x = \frac{135}{3} = 45$

5) Choice D is correct

We have two equations and three unknown variables, therefore x cannot be obtained.

6) Choice D is correct

Use distributive property to simplify $2(9y + 3)$ and $-3(2y + 2)$. Then:

$2(9x + 3) = 18y + 6$ and $-3(2y + 2) = -6y - 6$

Isolate the variable: $18y + 6 = -6y - 6$, subtract 6 from both sides.

$18y + 6 - 6 = -6y - 6 - 6 \rightarrow 18y = -6y - 12$, add $6y$ to both sides:

$18y + 6y = -6y - 12 + 6y \rightarrow 24y = -12$. Divide both sides by 24:

$$\rightarrow \frac{24y}{24} = \frac{-12}{24} \rightarrow y = -\frac{1}{2}$$

7) Choice B is correct

There is a small semicircle inside a big semicircle, then: the perimeter of big

semicircle $= \frac{8\times\pi}{2} = \frac{24}{2} = 12$ cm. The perimeter of small semicircle $= \frac{4\times\pi}{2} = \frac{12}{2} = 6$ cm

Total perimeter$= 4 + 6 + 12 = 22$ cm

8) Choice B is correct

Use FOIL (First-Out-In-Last) method to simplify the expression:

$(3x - 5)^2 = (3x - 5)(3x - 5) = 9x^2 - 15x - 15x + 25 = 9x^2 - 30x + 25$

9) Choice C is correct

$\frac{5}{2}x + \frac{1}{2}(2x + 1) - \frac{3}{2} = 3$, add $\frac{3}{2}$ to both sides: $\frac{5}{2}x + \frac{1}{2}(2x + 1) - \frac{3}{2} + \frac{3}{2} = 3 + \frac{3}{2}$. Simplify

$\frac{5}{2}x + \frac{1}{2}(2x + 1) = \frac{9}{2}$. Now, multiply both sides by 2: $\frac{5}{2}x + \frac{1}{2}(2x + 1) \times 2 = \frac{9}{2} \times 2$. Simplify

$5x + 2x + 1 = 9 \rightarrow 7x + 1 = 9$. Subtract 1 from both sides: $7x + 1 - 1 = 9 - 1$. Now,

simplify: $7x = 8$. Divide both sides by 7. Then: $\frac{7x}{7} = \frac{8}{7} \rightarrow x = \frac{8}{7}$

10) Choice B is correct

Base on triangle similarity theorem: $\frac{a}{a+b} = \frac{c}{3} \rightarrow c = \frac{3a}{a+b} = \frac{3\sqrt{2}}{3\sqrt{2}} = 1 \rightarrow$ The area of the

shaded region is: $\left(\frac{c+3}{2}\right)(b) = \frac{4}{2} \times 2\sqrt{2} = 4\sqrt{2}$.

11) Choice C is correct

Since this inequality contains absolute value, then, the value inside absolute value bars is greater than -4 and less than 4. Then:

$|x - 9| \leq 5 \rightarrow -5 \leq x - 9 \leq 5 \rightarrow -5 + 9 \leq x - 9 + 9 \leq 5 + 9 \rightarrow 4 \leq x \leq 14$

12) Choice C is correct

Set of numbers that are not composite between 1 and 20: $A = \{1, 2, 3, 5, 7, 11, 13, 17, 19\}$

$Probability = \dfrac{number\ of\ desired\ outcomes}{number\ of\ total\ outcomes} = \dfrac{9}{20}$

13) Choice D is correct

Let y be: $y = 4x - 3$. $average = \dfrac{sum\ of\ terms}{number\ of\ terms} \Rightarrow 10 = \dfrac{9+6+12+y+10}{5} \Rightarrow$

$10 = \dfrac{37 + y}{5} \Rightarrow (5 \times 10) = 37 + y \Rightarrow 50 = 37 + y \Rightarrow y = 50 - 37 = 13$

$$y = 4x - 3 \Rightarrow 13 = 4x - 3 \Rightarrow 4x = 13 + 3 \Rightarrow 4x = 16 \Rightarrow x = \frac{16}{4} = 4$$

14) Choice B is correct

Multiply both sides of the equation by s to clear the fraction resulting in $Cs = t - R$

Isolate the variable R, by adding R and subtracting Cs from both sides. This gives

$R = t - Cs$

15) Choice D is correct

The ratio of black cars to white cars is $3:8$. Therefore, there are 3 black cars out of 11 cars. To find the answer, first divide the total number of cars by 11, then multiply the result by 3. $66 \div 11 = 6 \Rightarrow 3 \times 6 = 18$. There are 18 black cars and 48 $(66 - 18)$ white cars. So, 30 more black cars should be added to make the ratio $1:1$.

16) Choice D is correct

Isolate and solve for y: $\frac{5}{8} - \frac{1}{4}y = \frac{1}{2} \rightarrow \frac{1}{4}y = \frac{5}{8} - \frac{1}{2} = \frac{1}{8} \rightarrow \frac{1}{4}y = \frac{1}{8}$

Multiply both sides by the reciprocal of the coefficient of y.

$$\left(\frac{4}{1}\right)\frac{1}{4}y = \frac{1}{8}\left(\frac{4}{1}\right) \rightarrow y = \frac{4}{8} = \frac{1}{2}$$

17) Choice D is correct

A. $x = 4 \rightarrow$ The perimeter of the figure is: $3 + 5 + 3 + 4 + 4 = 19 \neq 33$

B. $x = 6 \rightarrow$ The perimeter of the figure is: $3 + 5 + 3 + 6 + 6 = 23 \neq 33$

C. $x = 8 \rightarrow$ The perimeter of the figure is: $3 + 5 + 3 + 8 + 8 = 27 \neq 33$

D. $x = 11 \rightarrow$ The perimeter of the figure is: $3 + 5 + 3 + 11 + 11 = 33 = 33$

18) Choice D is correct

Use the FOIL (First, Out, In, Last) method to multiply two imaginary expressions:

$(-5)(-3) + (-5)(-13i) + (10i)(-3) + (10i)(-13i) = 15 + 65i - 30i - 130i^2$

Combine like terms $(+65i - 30i)$ and simplify:

$15 + 65i - 30i - 130i^2 = 15 + 35i - 130i^2$, $i^2 = -1$, then: $15 + 35i - 130i^2 =$
$15 + 35i - 130(-1) = 15 + 35i + 130 = 145 + 35i$

19) Choice B is correct

Plug in 140 for F and then solve for C.

$$C = \frac{5}{9}(F - 32) \Rightarrow C = \frac{5}{9}(140 - 32) \Rightarrow C = \frac{5}{9}(108) = 60$$

20) Choice D is correct

Simplify. $7x^2y^3(2x^2y)^3 = 7x^2y^3(8x^6y^3) = 56x^8y^6$

Accuplacer Mathematics Practice Test 4

Advanced Algebra and Functions

1) Choice B is correct

Since $B = 6$, substitute 6 for B in the equation $\frac{3y-6}{7} = B$, which gives $\frac{3y-6}{7} = 6$. Multiplying both sides of $\frac{3y-6}{7} = 6$ by 7 gives $3y - 6 = 42$ and then adding 6 to both sides of $3y - 6 = 42$ then, $3y = 48 \rightarrow y = \frac{48}{3} = 16$.

2) Choice A is correct

By definition, if $(b)^x = y$, where $b > 0$ and $b \neq 1$, then $x = \log_b y$. Therefore, the given equation $3^{2x} = 5$ can be rewritten in the form $\log_3 5 = 2x$. Next, solving for x by dividing both sides of the equation by 2 yields $x = \frac{\log_3 5}{2}$.

3) Choice A is correct

To solve for the side AC, we need to use sine of angle B. Then: $\sin \theta = \frac{opposite}{hypotenuse}$.
$\sin 55° = \frac{AC}{8} \rightarrow 8 \times \sin 55° = AC$. Now use a calculator to find $\sin 50°$.
$\sin 55° \approx 0.819$, $AC = 8 \times 0.819 = 6.552$, rounding to the nearest tenth: $6.552 \approx 6.6$

4) Choice C is correct

To rewrite $\frac{2+3i}{5-2i}$ in the standard form $a + bi$, multiply the numerator and denominator of $\frac{2+3i}{5-2i}$ by the conjugate, $5 + 2i$. This gives $\left(\frac{2+3i}{5-2i}\right)\left(\frac{5+2i}{5+2i}\right) = \frac{10+4i+15i+6i^2}{5^2-(2i)^2}$. Since $i^2 = -1$, this last fraction can be rewritten as $\frac{10+4i+15i+6(-1)}{25-4(-1)} = \frac{4+19i}{29}$.

5) Choice A is correct

In a rational function, if the denominator has a bigger degree than the numerator, the horizontal asymptote is the x-axes or the line $y = 0$. In the function $f(x) = \frac{x+2}{x^2+1}$, the degree of numerator is 1 (x to the power of 1) and the degree of the denominator is 2 (x to the power of 2). Then, the horizontal asymptote is the line $y = 0$.

6) Choice D is correct

Multiplying each side of $-3x - y = 6$ by 2 gives $-6x - 2y = 12$. Adding each side of $-6x - 2y = 12$ to the corresponding side of $6x + 4y = 10$ gives $2y = 22$ or $y = 11$. Finally, substituting 11 for y in $6x + 4y = 10$ gives $6x + 4(11) = 10 \rightarrow$

$6x = 10 - 44 \rightarrow 6x = -34$ or $x = -\frac{17}{3}$. $(x, y) = \left(-\frac{17}{3}, 11\right)$. So, choice D is correct.

7) Choice A is correct

Identify the input value. Since the function is in the form $f(x)$ and the question asks to calculate $f(3)$, the input value is three. $f(3) \rightarrow x = 3$. Using the function, input the desired x value. Now substitute 3 in for every x in the function. $f(x) = 3x^2 - 4$,

$f(3) = 3(3)^2 - 4 \rightarrow f(3) = 27 - 4 \rightarrow f(3) = 23$

8) Choice D is correct

The problem asks for the sum of the roots of the quadratic equation

$2n^2 + 16n + 24 = 0$. Dividing each side of the equation by 2 gives $n^2 + 8n + 12 = 0$. If the roots of $n^2 + 8n + 12 = 0$ are n_1 and n_2, then the equation can be factored as

$n^2 + 8n + 12 = (n - n_1)(n - n_2) = 0$. Looking at the coefficient of n on each side of

$n^2 + 8n + 12 = (n + 6)(n + 2)$ gives $n = -6$ or $n = -2$, then, $-6 + (-2) = -8$

9) Choice A is correct

The graph of $y = f(x)$ crosses the x-axis at $x = -3$ and $x = 1$, and crosses the y-axis at $y = -3$, and has its vertex at the point $(-1, -4)$. Therefore, the ordered pairs $(-3, 0)$, $(1, 0)$, $(0, -3)$, and $(-1, -4)$ must satisfy the equation for $f(x)$. Furthermore, because the graph opens upward, the equation defining $f(x)$ must have positive leading coefficient. All of these conditions are met by the equation:

$f(x) = x^2 + 2x - 3$

10) Choice D is correct

The sum of two supplementary angles is 180 degrees. Then:

$(3x - 10) + (x + 2) = 180$. Simplify and solve for x: $(3x - 10) + (x + 2) = 180 \rightarrow$

$$4x - 8 = 180 \rightarrow 4x = 180 + 8 \rightarrow 4x = 188 \rightarrow x = 47$$

11) Choice C is correct

If $x - a$ is a factor of $g(x)$, then $g(a)$ must equal 0. Based on the table $g(1) = 0$. Therefore, $x - 1$ must be a factor of $g(x)$.

12) Choice C is correct

To solve this problem first solve the equation for c. Then: $\frac{c}{b} = 2$. Multiply by b on both sides. Then: $b \times \frac{c}{b} = 2 \times b \rightarrow c = 2b$. Now to calculate $\frac{6b}{c}$, substitute the value for c into the denominator and simplify. $\frac{6b}{c} = \frac{6b}{2b} = \frac{6}{2} = 3$

13) Choice B is correct

Simplify the numerator: $\frac{x+(5x)^2+(3x)^3}{x} = \frac{x+5^2x^2+3^3x^3}{x} = \frac{x+25x^2+27x^3}{x}$. Pull an x out of each term in the numerator. $\frac{x(1+25x+27x^2)}{x}$. The x in the numerator and the x in the denominator cancel: $1 + 25x + 27x^2 = 27x^2 + 25x + 1$

14) Choice A is correct

The equation $\frac{c-b}{c} = \frac{24}{27}$ can be rewritten as $\frac{c}{c} - \frac{b}{c} = \frac{24}{27}$, from which it follows that $1 - \frac{b}{c} = \frac{24}{27}$, or $\frac{b}{c} = 1 - \frac{24}{27} = \frac{1}{9}$

15) Choice A is correct

First write the equation in slope intercept form. Add $3x$ to both sides to get $5y = 3x + 45$. Now divide both sides by 5 to get $y = \frac{3}{5}x + 9$. The slope of this line is $\frac{3}{5}$, so any line that also has a slope of $\frac{3}{5}$ would be parallel to it. Only choice A has a slope of $\frac{3}{5}$.

16) Choice D is correct

To find the average of three numbers even if they're algebraic expressions, add them up and divide by 3. Thus, the average equals: $\frac{(4x+2)+(-6x-5)+(8x+2)}{3} = \frac{6x-1}{3} = 2x - \frac{1}{3}$

17) Choice C is correct

Let l and w be the length and width, respectively, of the original rectangle. The area of the original rectangle is $A = lw$. The rectangle is altered by increasing its length by 20 percent and decreasing its width by s percent; thus, the length of the altered rectangle is $1.2l$, and the width of the altered rectangle is $\left(1 - \frac{s}{100}\right)w$. The alterations decrease the area by 4 percent, so the area of the altered rectangle is $(1 - 0.04)A = 0.96A$. The altered rectangle is the product of its length and width, therefore $0.96A = (1.2l)(1 - \frac{s}{100})w$. Since $A = lw$, this equation can be rewritten as $0.96A = (1.2)\left(1 - \frac{s}{100}\right)lw = (1.2)(1 - \frac{s}{100})A$, from which it follows that

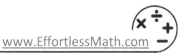

$0.96 = (1.2)\left(1 - \frac{s}{100}\right)$, divide both sides of the equation by 1.2. Then: $0.8 = 1 - \frac{s}{100}$
Therefore, $\frac{s}{100} = 0.2$ and therefore the value of s is 20.

18) Choice B is correct

Because each children ticket costs $3 and each adult ticket costs $4, the total amount, in dollars, that John spends on x student tickets and 2 adult ticket is $3(x) + 4(2)$. Because John spends at least $10 but no more than $15 on the tickets, you can write the compound inequality $3x + 8 \geq 10$ and $3x + 8 \leq 15$. Subtracting 8 from each side of both inequalities and then dividing each side of both inequalities by 3 gives

$x \geq 0.66$ and $x \leq 2.3$. Thus, the value of x must be an integer that is both greater than or equal to 0.66 and less than or equal to 2.3. Therefore, $x = 1$ or $x = 2$. Either 1 or 2 may be chosen as the correct answer.

19) Choice B is correct

The sum of all angles in a quadrilateral is 360 degrees. Let x be the smallest angle in the quadrilateral. Then the angles are: $x, 4x, 6x, 7x$

$x + 4x + 6x + 7x = 360 \rightarrow 8x = 360 \rightarrow x = 20$. The angles in the quadrilateral are: $20°, 80°, 120°,$ and $140°$.

20) Choice D is correct

To find the vertical asymptote(s) of a rational function, set the denominator equal to 0 and solve for x. Then: $3x + 5 = 0 \rightarrow 3x = -5 \rightarrow x = -\frac{5}{3}$.

The vertical asymptote is $x = -\frac{5}{3}$.

ACCUPLACER Mathematical Reasoning Practice Test 5

Arithmetic

1) Choice A is correct

Use order of operation rule (PEMDAS). First, simplify inside the parenthesis:

$17[23 - (1 + 2)^2] = 17[23 - 9] = 17[14] = 238$

2) Choice B is correct

The population is increased by 10% and 25%. 10% increase changes the population to 110% of original population. For the second increase, multiply the result by 125%.

$(1.10) \times (1.25) = 1.375 = 137.5\%$. 37.5 percent of population is increased after two years.

3) Choice D is correct

To multiply two numbers in scientific notation, multiply their coefficients and add their exponents. For these two numbers in scientific notation, multiply the coefficients: $1.7 \times 2.3 = 3.91$. Add the powers of 10: $10^9 \times 10^{-7} = 10^{9+(-7)} = 10^2$. Then:

$(1.7 \times 10^9) \times (2.3 \times 10^{-7}) = (1.7 \times 2.3) \times (10^9 \times 10^{-7}) = 3.91 \times (10^{9+(-7)})$

$= 3.91 \times 10^2$

4) Choice C is correct

$5 \text{ percent of } 460 = \dfrac{5}{100} \times 460 = \dfrac{1}{20} \times 460 = \dfrac{460}{20} = 23$

5) Choice B is correct

1,000 times a number is 40.5. Let x be the number, then: $1,000x = 40.5 \rightarrow$

$x = \dfrac{40.5}{1,000} = 0.0405$

6) Choice A is correct

$59,767,544.5 \times \dfrac{1}{100,000} = 597.675445$

7) Choice C is correct

$\dfrac{6}{15} - \dfrac{4}{30} = \dfrac{12}{30} - \dfrac{4}{30} = \dfrac{8}{30} = \dfrac{4}{15}$

8) Choice A is correct

Let's review the choices:

A. $0.2\% < \frac{1}{20}$. This is a correct statement. $2\% = 0.02$ and $\frac{1}{20} = 0.05 \rightarrow 0.02 < 0.05$.

B. $\frac{7}{8} < 0.8$. This is not a correct statement. Because 0.8 is less than $\frac{7}{8} = 0.875$

C. $3.5 < \frac{7}{3}$. This is not a correct statement. Because $\frac{7}{3} = 2.33$ and it's less than 3.5.

D. $\frac{2}{6} > \frac{3}{8}$. This is a not a correct statement. Because $\frac{2}{6} = 0.33$ and it's less than

$\frac{3}{8} = 0.375$.

9) Choice C is correct

18% of $150 = \frac{18}{100} \times 150 = 27$. Let x be the number, then, $x = 35 + 27 = 62$

10) Choice A is correct

Only choice A is equal to 87. $\left(9 \times \frac{8}{2}\right) + \left(\frac{2}{8} \times 4\right) + 50 = (9 \times 4) + \left(\frac{1}{4} \times 4\right) + 50 =$

$36 + 1 + 50 = 87$

11) Choice B is correct

The result when 859 is divided by 9 is 95 with a remainder of 4. Multiplying

$9 \times 95 = 855$ and $859 - 855 = 4$

12) Choice D is correct

Dividing 90 by 15%, which is equivalent to 0.15, gives 600.

13) Choice D is correct

$0.05A$ is equal to 5% A. Only choice D is not equal to 50 percent of A.

14) Choice B is correct

Use simple interest formula: $I = prt$ (I = interest, p = principal, r = rate, t = time)

$I = 8,700 - 7,500 = 1,200$, $t = 2$, $p = \$7,500$

$1,200 = (7,500)(r)(2) \Rightarrow 1200 = (15,000)(r) \Rightarrow r = \dfrac{1,200}{15,000} = 0.08 \times 100 = 8\%$

15) Choice A is correct

Digit 2 is in the tenths place. Then, the value of 2 in 851.251 is 0.2 or 2 tenths.

16) Choice D is correct

$$\frac{6}{4}+\frac{4}{8}+\frac{3}{2}=\frac{12+4+12}{8}=\frac{28}{8}=\frac{7}{2}$$

17) Choice D is correct

Number of packs equal to: $\frac{22}{4}=5.5$. Therefore, the school must purchase 6 packs.

18) Choice C is correct

Number 0.00095 is equal to 9.5×10^{-4} in scientific notation.

19) Choice D is correct

$$12.124 \div 0.002 = \frac{\frac{12,124}{1,000}}{\frac{2}{1,000}} = \frac{12,124}{2} = 6,062$$

20) Choice C is correct

The fraction $\frac{4}{5}$ can be written as $\frac{4\times20}{5\times20}=\frac{80}{100}$, which can be interpreted as eighty hundredths, or 0.80.

Accuplacer Mathematics Practice Test 5

Quantitative Reasoning, Algebra, and Statistics

1) Choice A is correct

The length of MN is equal to: $3x + 5x = 8x$. Then: $8x = 40 \rightarrow x = \frac{40}{8} = 5$

The length of ON is equal to: $5x = 5 \times 5 = 25\ cm$

2) Choice D is correct

A. $x = \frac{1}{2} \rightarrow \frac{5}{9} + \frac{1}{2} = \frac{10+9}{18} = \frac{19}{18} \approx 1.056 < 2$

B. $x = \frac{3}{5} \rightarrow \frac{5}{9} + \frac{3}{5} = \frac{25+27}{45} = \frac{52}{45} \approx 1.16 < 2$

C. $x = \frac{4}{5} \rightarrow \frac{5}{9} + \frac{4}{5} = \frac{25+36}{45} = \frac{61}{45} \approx 1.36 < 2$

D. $x = \frac{5}{3} \rightarrow \frac{5}{9} + \frac{5}{3} = \frac{5+15}{9} = \frac{20}{9} \approx 2.2 > 2$

Only Choice D can be the value of x.

3) Choice A is correct

Substitute 6 for a and -3 for b in the equation to get $\frac{6^2-(-3)^2}{6-(-3)}$. Following order of operations, $\frac{6^2-(-3)^2}{6-(-3)} = \frac{36-9}{9} = \frac{27}{9} = 3$

4) Choice C is correct

Write the ratio of $5a$ to $2b$. $\frac{5a}{2b} = \frac{1}{10}$. Use cross multiplication and then simplify.

$5a \times 10 = 2b \times 1 \rightarrow 50a = 2b \rightarrow a = \frac{2b}{50} = \frac{b}{25}$. Now, find the ratio of a to b:

$\frac{a}{b} = \frac{\frac{b}{25}}{b} \rightarrow \frac{b}{25} \div b = \frac{b}{25} \times \frac{1}{b} = \frac{b}{25b} = \frac{1}{25}$. The ratio of a to b is 1 to 25 or $\frac{1}{25}$.

5) Choice D is correct

$0.6x = (0.3) \times 20 \rightarrow x = 10 \rightarrow (x + 5)^2 = (10 + 5)^2 = (15)^2 = 225$

6) Choice A is correct

The formula for factoring the difference of two squares is $a^2 - b^2 = (a - b)(a + b)$. Here, $x^2 - 9 = x^2 - 3^2$. Replacing a with x and b with 4 gives $(x - 3)(x + 3)$.

7) Choice B is correct

Given the two equations, substitute the numerical value of a into the second equation to solve for m. $a = \sqrt{2}$, $3a = \sqrt{3m}$. Substituting the numerical value for a into the equation with x is as follows. $3(\sqrt{2}) = \sqrt{3m}$. From here, distribute the 3.

$3\sqrt{2} = \sqrt{3m}$. Now square both side of the equation. $(3\sqrt{2})^2 = (\sqrt{3m})^2$. Remember to square both terms within the parentheses. Also, recall that squaring a square root sign cancels them out. $3^2\sqrt{2}^2 = 3m \rightarrow 9(2) = 3m \rightarrow 18 = 3m \rightarrow m = 6$

8) Choice D is correct

We have two equations and three unknown variables, therefore x cannot be obtained.

9) Choice D is correct

$16 - \frac{2}{5}x \geq 8$. Subtract 16 from both side: $16 - \frac{2}{5}x - 16 \geq 8 - 16$. Now, simplify:

$-\frac{2}{5}x \geq -8$ multiply both sides by $-\frac{5}{2}$ (revers the inequality):

$\left(-\frac{5}{2}\right)\left(-\frac{2}{5}x\right) \leq (-8)\left(-\frac{5}{2}\right) \rightarrow \frac{10x}{10} \leq \frac{40}{2} \rightarrow x \leq 20$.

10) Choice B is correct

First, find a common denominator for 2 and $\frac{3x}{x-5}$. It's $x - 5$. Then:

$2 + \frac{3x}{x-5} = \frac{2(x-5)}{x-5} + \frac{3x}{x-5} = \frac{2x-10+3x}{x-5} = \frac{5x-10}{x-5}$. Now, multiply the numerator and denominator of $\frac{3}{5-x}$ by -1. Then: $\frac{3\times(-1)}{(5-x)\times(-1)} = \frac{-3}{x-5}$. Rewrite the expression: $\frac{5x-10}{x-5} = \frac{-3}{x-5}$. Since the denominators of both fractions are equal, then, the numerators must be equal. $5x - 10 = -3 \rightarrow 5x = 7 \rightarrow x = \frac{7}{5}$.

11) Choice D is correct

$y = 2ab + 3b^3$. Plug in the values of a and b in the equation: $a = 3$ and $b = 5$

$y = 2(3)(5) + 3(5)^3 = 30 + 3(125) = 30 + 375 = 405$

12) Choice A is correct

To write this expression as a single fraction, we need to find a common denominator. The common denominator of $9b$ and $6b$ is $18b$. Then:

$-2 + \frac{3b-4c}{9b} - \frac{2b+2c}{6b} = \frac{-2(18b)}{18b} + \frac{2(3b-4c)}{18b} - \frac{3(2b+2c)}{18b}$. Now, simplify the numerators and combine: $\frac{-2(18b)}{18b} + \frac{2(3b-4c)}{18b} - \frac{3(2b+2c)}{18b} = \frac{-36b}{18b} + \frac{6b-8c}{18b} - \frac{6b+6c}{18b} = \frac{-36b+6b-8c-6b-6c}{18b} = \frac{-36b-14c}{18b}$

Divide both numerator and denominator by 2. Then: $\frac{-36b-14c}{18b} = \frac{-18b-7c}{9b}$

13) Choice D is correct

Let put some values for a and b. If $a = 9$ and $b = 2 \rightarrow a \times b = 18 \rightarrow \frac{18}{3} = 6 \rightarrow 18$ is divisible by 3. Let's review the choices:

A. $3a - b = (3 \times 9) - 2 = 27 - 2 = 25$ is not divisible by 3.

B. If $a = 11$ and $b = 3 \rightarrow a \times b = 33 \rightarrow \frac{33}{3} = 11$ and $a - 3b = 11 - (3 \times 3) = 11 - 9 = 2$ is not divisible by 3.

C. $\frac{a}{b} = \frac{11}{3}$ is not divisible by 3.

D. $4 \times a \times b \rightarrow 4 \times 11 \times 3 = 132$. It is divisible by 3. If you choose any other numbers for a and b you will get the same result.

14) Choice B is correct

The area of the floor is: $6 \ cm \times 24 \ cm = 144 \ cm^2$. The number of tiles needed =

$144 \div 8 = 18$

15) Choice B is correct

To solve for a, first use distributive property to simplify $8(a + 8)$. Then:

$8(a + 8) = 8a + 64$. Now, combine like terms: $-3a + 8(a + 8) = 49 \rightarrow$

$-3a + 8a + 64 = 49 \rightarrow 5a + 64 = 49$. Subtract 64 from both sides: $5a + 64 - 64 =$

$49 - 64 \rightarrow 5a = -15 \rightarrow a = -3$

16) Choice D is correct

$\frac{25}{A} + 1 = 6 \rightarrow \frac{25}{A} = 6 - 1 = 5 \rightarrow 25 = 5A \rightarrow A = \frac{25}{5} = 5$. Then: $25 + A = 25 + 5 = 30$

17) Choice B is correct

The area of the triangle: $\frac{6 \times 8}{2} = 24$, the area of the rectangle: $6 \times 10 = 60$. The fraction of the shaded part is: $\frac{24}{60} = \frac{2}{5}$

18) Choice D is correct

Let b be the amount of time Alec needs to do the job, then:

$\frac{1}{a} + \frac{1}{b} = \frac{1}{100} \rightarrow \frac{1}{300} + \frac{1}{b} = \frac{1}{100} \rightarrow \frac{1}{b} = \frac{1}{100} - \frac{1}{300} = \frac{2}{300} = \frac{1}{150}$. Then: $b = 150$ minutes

19) Choice B is correct

First square both sides of the equation to get $6n - 5 = n^2$. Subtracting both sides by $6n - 5$ gives us the equation $n^2 - 6n + 5 = 0$. Here you can solve the quadratic equation by factoring to get $(n - 1)(n - 5) = 0$. For the expression $(n - 1)(n - 5)$ to equal zero, $n = 1$ or $n = 5$.

20) Choice D is correct

Use fractions division rule: $\frac{a}{b} \div \frac{c}{d} = \frac{a}{b} \times \frac{d}{c} = \frac{a \times d}{b \times c}$. Then: $\frac{7x}{x+4} \div \frac{x}{2x+8} = \frac{7x}{x+4} \times \frac{2x+8}{x} = \frac{7x(2x+8)}{x(x+4)} = \frac{7x \times 2(x+4)}{x(x+4)}$. Cancel common factor: $\frac{7x \times 2(x+4)}{x(x+4)} = \frac{14x(x+4)}{x(x+4)} = 14$.

Accuplacer Mathematics Practice Test 5

Advanced Algebra and Functions

1) Choice D is correct

Solve for x: $x^3 + 18 = 130 \rightarrow x^3 = 112$. Let's review the choices.

A. 1 and 2. $1^3 = 1$ and $2^3 = 8$, 112 is not between these two numbers.

B. 2 and 3. $2^3 = 8$ and $3^3 = 27$, 112 is not between these two numbers.

C. 3 and 4. $3^3 = 27$ and $4^3 = 64$, 112 is not between these two numbers.

D. 4 and 5. $4^3 = 64$ and $5^3 = 125$, 112 is between these two numbers.

2) Choice B is correct

Solve for y: $\frac{3y}{25} = \frac{y-1}{5}$. Multiply the second fraction by 5: $\frac{3y}{25} = \frac{5(y-1)}{5 \times 5}$

Two denominators are equal. Therefore, the numerators must be equal.

$3y = 5y - 5 \rightarrow -2y = -5 \rightarrow y = \dfrac{5}{2}$

3) Choice D is correct

$(x-2)^3 = 27 \rightarrow \sqrt[3]{(x-2)^3} = \sqrt[3]{27} \rightarrow x - 2 = 3 \rightarrow x = 5 \rightarrow (x-6)(x-4)$
$$= (5-6)(5-4) = (-1)(1) = -1$$

4) Choice D is correct

The cotangent is the reciprocal of tangent: $tangent\ a = \dfrac{1}{cotangent\ a} = \dfrac{1}{2}$

5) Choice B is correct

To solve for x, isolate the radical on one side of the equation. Divide both sides by 4.

Then: $4\sqrt{2x+9} = 28 \rightarrow \frac{4\sqrt{2x+9}}{4} = \frac{28}{4} \rightarrow \sqrt{2x+9} = 7$. Square both sides:

$\left(\sqrt{(2x+9)}\right)^2 = 7^2$. Then: $2x + 9 = 49 \rightarrow 2x = 40 \rightarrow x = 20$. Substitute x by 20 in the

original equation and check the answer: $x = 20 \rightarrow 4\sqrt{2(20)+9} = 4\sqrt{49} = 4(7) = 28$

6) Choice D is correct

Solve the system of equations by elimination method.

$\begin{array}{l} 3x - 4y = -20 \\ -x + 2y = 10 \end{array}$ Multiply the second equation by 3, then add it to the first equation.

$$3x - 4y = -20 \quad 3x - 4y = -20$$
$$3(-x + 2y = 10) \Rightarrow -3x + 6y = 30 \Rightarrow \text{add the equations } 2y = 10 \Rightarrow y = 5$$

7) Choice A is correct

Since $f(x)$ is linear function with a negative slop, then when $x = -3$, $f(x)$ is maximum and when $x = 2$, $f(x)$ is minimum. Then the ratio of the minimum value to the maximum value of the function is: $\frac{f(2)}{f(-3)} = \frac{-2(2)+1}{-2(-3)+1} = \frac{-3}{7} = -\frac{3}{7}$.

8) Choice D is correct

Frist factor the function: $f(x) = x^3 + 8x^2 + 12x = x(x + 2)(x + 6)$, To find the zeros, $f(x)$ should be zero. $f(x) = x(x + 2)(x + 6) = 0$. Therefore, the zeros are: $x = 0$, $(x + 2) = 0 \Rightarrow x = -2$, $(x + 6) = 0 \Rightarrow x = -6$

9) Choice C is correct

Here we can substitute 6 for x in the equation. Thus, $y - 2 = 3(6 + 2)$, $y - 2 = 24$,

Adding 2 to both side of the equation: $y = 24 + 2 \rightarrow y = 26$

The y-coordinate of A is 26.

10) Choice D is correct

In the figure, angle A is labeled $(3x - 8)$ and it measures 49. Thus,

$3x - 8 = 49$ and $3x = 57$ or $x = 19$. That means that angle B, which is labeled $(4x)$, must measure $4 \times 19 = 76$. Since the three angles of a triangle must add up to 180,

$49 + 76 + y - 9 = 180$, then: $y + 116 = 180 \rightarrow y = 180 - 116 = 64$.

11) Choice C is correct

If $x - a$ is a factor of $g(x)$, then $g(a)$ must equal 0. Based on the table

$g(-2) = 0$. Therefore, $x - (-2)$ or $x + 2$ must be a factor of $g(x)$.

12) Choice C is correct

If $f(x) = g(x)$, then: $\ln(f(x)) = \ln(g(x)) \rightarrow \ln(e^{3x}) = \ln(18)$. Use logarithm rule: $\log_a x^b = b \log_a x \rightarrow \ln(e^{3x}) = 3x \ln(e) \rightarrow (3x) \ln(e) = \ln(18)$

$\ln(e) = 1$, then: $(3x)\ln(e) = \ln(18) \rightarrow 3x = \ln(18) \rightarrow x = \frac{\ln(18)}{3}$

13) Choice B is correct

Convert mixed numbers to fractions and simplify:

$$\frac{\left(\frac{1}{4} + 1\frac{1}{3} - 1\frac{1}{2}\right)}{\left(2\frac{1}{3} + 1\frac{1}{3} - 3\frac{1}{3}\right)} = \frac{\frac{1}{4} + \frac{4}{3} - \frac{3}{2}}{\frac{7}{3} + \frac{4}{3} - \frac{10}{3}} = \frac{\frac{3+16-18}{12}}{\frac{1}{3}} = \frac{\frac{1}{12}}{\frac{1}{3}} = \frac{1 \times 3}{12 \times 1} = \frac{3}{12} = \frac{1}{4} = 0.25$$

14) Choice C is correct

Apply the absolute rule: $x + 5 \leq -2$ or $x + 5 \geq 2$

$x + 5 \leq -2 \rightarrow x \leq -5 - 2 \rightarrow x \leq -7, x + 5 \geq 2 \rightarrow x \geq 2 - 5 \rightarrow x \geq -3$

Combine the intervals: $x \leq -7 \; or \; x \geq -3$.

15) Choice A is correct

The equation of a circle in standard form is: $(x - h)^2 + (y - k)^2 = r^2$, where the center is at: (h, k) and its radius is: r, Then, for the circle with equation

$(x - 3)^2 + (y + 5)^2 = 5$, the center is at $(3, -5)$ and its radius is $\sqrt{5}$ $(r^2 = 5 \rightarrow r = \sqrt{5})$

16) Choice C is correct

To find the average of four numbers even if they're algebraic expressions, add them up and divide by 4 thus, the average equals: $\frac{(2y+4)+(4y-3)+(-y+3)+(3y-1)}{4} = \frac{8y+3}{4} = 2y + \frac{3}{4}$

17) Choice A is correct

$\left(\frac{f}{g}\right)(x) = \frac{f(x)}{g(x)} = \frac{7x - 5}{2x^2 - 4x}$

18) Choice A is correct

In the function $f(x) = \frac{4x^2 - 6x + 12}{9 - x}$, the denominator cannot be zero. Then, $9 - x \neq 0 \rightarrow x \neq 9$. So, $f(9)$ is not defined.

19) Choice A is correct

$(x + 2)(x + p) = x^2 + (2 + p)x + 2p \rightarrow 2 + p = 6 \rightarrow p = 4 \; and \; r = 2p = 8$

20) Choice B is correct.

Simplify the expression. $\sqrt{\frac{x^2}{2} + \frac{x^2}{16}} = \sqrt{\frac{8x^2}{16} + \frac{x^2}{16}} = \sqrt{\frac{9x^2}{16}} = \sqrt{\frac{9}{16}x^2} = \sqrt{\frac{9}{16}} \times \sqrt{x^2} = \frac{3}{4} \times x = \frac{3x}{4}$

Receive the PDF version of this book or get another FREE book!

Thank you for using our Book!

Do you LOVE this book?

Then, you can get the PDF version of this book or another book absolutely FREE!

Please email us at:

info@EffortlessMath.com

for details.

Author's Final Note

I hope you enjoyed reading this book. You've made it through the book! Great job!

First of all, thank you for purchasing this practice book. I know you could have picked any number of books to help you prepare for your Accuplacer Math test, but you picked this book and for that I am extremely grateful.

It took me years to write this practice book for the Accuplacer Math because I wanted to prepare a comprehensive Accuplacer Math book to help test takers make the most effective use of their valuable time while preparing for the test.

After teaching and tutoring math courses for over a decade, I've gathered my personal notes and lessons to develop this practice test. It is my greatest hope that the practice tests in this book could help you prepare for your test successfully.

If you have any questions, please contact me at reza@effortlessmath.com and I will be glad to assist. Your feedback will help me to greatly improve the quality of my books in the future and make this book even better. Furthermore, I expect that I have made a few minor errors somewhere in this book. If you think this to be the case, please let me know so I can fix the issue as soon as possible.

If you enjoyed this book and found some benefit in reading this, I'd like to hear from you and hope that you could take a quick minute to post a review on the book's Amazon page. To leave your valuable feedback, please visit: amzn.to/3mueFSx

Or scan this QR code.

I personally go over every single review, to make sure my books really are reaching out and helping students and test takers. Please help me help Accuplacer Math test takers, by leaving a review!

I wish you all the best in your future success!

Reza Nazari

Math teacher and author

Made in the USA
Columbia, SC
05 May 2021